HOW TO COUNSEL

In this Series

How to Apply for a Job
How to Apply to an Industrial Tribunal
How to Be a Freelance Journalist
How to Be a Freelance Secretary
How to Be a Local Councillor
How to Be an Effective School Governor
How to Become an Au Pair
How to Buy & Run a Shop
How to Buy & Run a Small Hotel
How to Choose a Private School
How to Claim State Benefits
How to Communicate at Work
How to Conduct Staff Appraisals
How to Counsel People at Work
How to Do Voluntary Work Abroad
How to Do Your Own Advertising
How to Emigrate
How to Employ & Manage Staff
How to Enjoy Retirement
How to Find Temporary Work Abroad
How to Get a Job Abroad
How to Get a Job in America
How to Get a Job in Australia
How to Get a Job in Europe
How to Get a Job in France
How to Get a Job in Germany
How to Get a Job in Hotels & Catering
How to Get a Job in Travel & Tourism
How to Get Into Films & TV
How to Get Into Radio
How to Get That Job
How to Help Your Child at School
How to Invest in Stocks & Shares
How to Keep Business Accounts
How to Know Your Rights at Work
How to Know Your Rights: Students
How to Know Your Rights: Teachers
How to Live & Work in America
How to Live & Work in Australia
How to Live & Work in Belgium
How to Live & Work in France
How to Live & Work in Germany
How to Live & Work in Hong Kong
How to Live & Work in Italy
How to Live & Work in Japan
How to Live & Work in New Zealand
How to Live & Work in Portugal
How to Live & Work in Saudi Arabia
How to Live & Work in Spain
How to Live & Work in the Gulf
How to Lose Weight & Keep Fit
How to Make a Wedding Speech
How to Manage a Sales Team
How to Manage Budgets & Cash Flows
How to Manage Computers at Work
How to Manage People at Work
How to Manage Your Career
How to Master Book-Keeping
How to Master Business English
How to Master GCSE Accounts
How to Master Languages
How to Master Public Speaking
How to Pass Exams Without Anxiety
How to Pass That Interview
How to Plan a Wedding
How to Prepare Your Child for School
How to Publish a Book
How to Publish a Newsletter
How to Raise Business Finance
How to Raise Funds & Sponsorship
How to Rent & Buy Property in France
How to Rent & Buy Property in Italy
How to Retire Abroad
How to Return to Work
How to Run a Local Campaign
How to Run a Voluntary Group
How to Sell Your Business
How to Spend a Year Abroad
How to Start a Business from Home
How to Start a New Career
How to Start Your Own Business
How to Start Word Processing
How to Study Abroad
How to Study & Learn
How to Study & Live in Britain
How to Survive at College
How to Survive Divorce
How to Take Care of Your Heart
How to Teach Abroad
How to Travel Round the World
How to Understand Finance at Work
How to Use a Library
How to Work from Home
How to Work in an Office
How to Work with Dogs
How to Write a Press Release
How to Write a Report
How to Write an Assignment
How to Write an Essay
How to Write Business Letters
How to Write for Publication
How to Write for Television

Other titles in preparation

COUNSEL PEOPLE AT WORK

A practical approach to Staff Care

John Humphries
Member, British Association for Counselling

How To Books

By the same author in this series
How to Manage People at Work

British Library Cataloguing in Publication Data
A catalogue record for this book is available from the British Library.

First published in 1995 by How To Books Ltd, Plymbridge House,
Estover Road, Plymouth PL6 7PZ, United Kingdom.
Tel: (01752) 735251/695745. Fax: (01752) 695699. Telex: 45635.

Note: The material contained in this book is set out in good faith for general guidance and no liability can be accepted for loss or expense incurred as a result of relying in particular circumstances on statements made in the book. The laws and regulations are complex and liable to change, and readers should check the current position with the relevant authorities before making personal arrangements.

Typeset by PDQ Typesetting, Stoke-on-Trent
Printed and bound by The Cromwell Press, Broughton Gifford, Melksham, Wiltshire.

Contents

List of Illustrations

IS THIS YOU?

Office manager

Personnel officer

Trainer

Sports coach

Medical doctor

Consultant

Probation officer

Mentor

Solicitor

Youth leader

Sales manager

Retailer

Company director

Accountant

Nurse

Social worker

Tutor

Advisor

Holiday courier

Police officer

Physiotherapist

Personnel manager

Supervisor

Scouter/Guider

Occupational therapist

Hotel manager

Priest

Lawyer

Works manager

Carer

Trade union official

Military officer

Department head

School teacher

Friend

Professional counsellor

Fig. 1. Is this you? People in a wide variety of roles may find themselves required to provide counselling.

Preface

From the earliest times people have experienced crises, difficulties and upsets of every conceivable kind. These were often caused by the impact of such events as war, crop failure and religious persecution and much of the population countered these problems by moving away.

With the advent of the industrial revolution, many people were forced off the land to live in overcrowded dismal urban conditions which brought a whole range of new problems and pressures in their wake. Again, escapism – this time in the form of emigration to the United States and elsewhere – proved the solution for many.

As the years progressed, and the pace of change has accelerated, people have had to endure more social pressures than ever before. Few would disagree that we are now living in times of stress without parallel. However, we can no longer avoid these stresses by simply moving away, as we live in a more formalised society and there are simply fewer stress-free places to move to.

What are the causes of this modern increase in stress? Many psychologists and psychiatrists have put forward theories in an attempt to explain them. Is it the increases in population throughout the world with the resultant fierce competition for scarce land and resources? Is it improved communications bringing the world's problems into our front rooms? Is it the consumer society encouraging us to buy more than we need or can afford? Is it economic circumstances causing redundancies to many and increased work loads for others? Is it the explosive increase in technology over the last 25 years bringing its own problems of change in working methods and habits? It is probably a combination of all these.

We are all affected by different causes in different ways. How can we cope with these pressures? Although we can no longer avoid or ignore them, some people seek escape in drugs and alcohol, which only generate their own additional problems. Other turn to crime and violence as a means of expressing their frustrations. Fortunately, more people are learning to seek help from others and this is where counselling has an increasingly vital role to play.

Counselling provides a means whereby people can talk through their problem with someone not directly involved, but who can help the person towards acceptable solutions.

This book is not intended to turn the reader into a professional counsellor. However, hopefully the counselling techniques described will help you to play your part when you find yourself in a counselling role either at work or in other social settings.

John Humphries

1
What is Counselling?

DEFINITIONS

'Advice – often asked for but rarely accepted.'

Counselling is the process of helping another person to find and act upon a solution to their problem.

The person conducting the counselling is known as the **counsellor** and the one being counselled is referred to as the **counsellee** or **client.**

FOUR BASIC STYLES OF HELPING

There are of four basic styles of helping as illustrated in the following diagram:

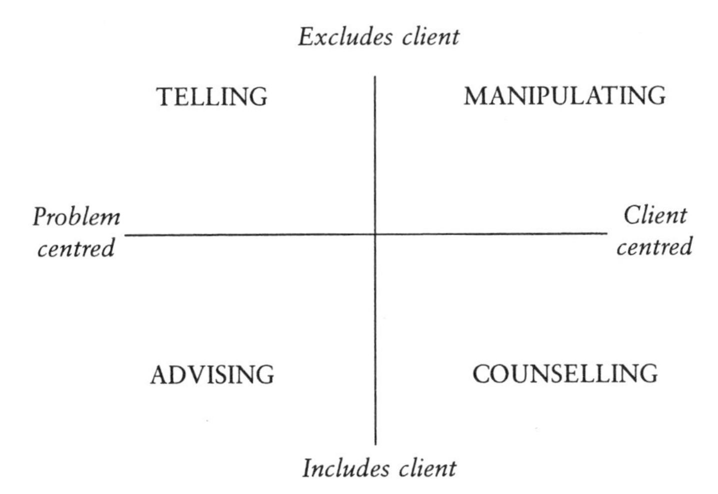

Fig 2. The four basic styles of helping.

The four styles are:

- telling
- manipulating
- advising
- counselling.

Let us consider each in more detail.

The helper who 'tells'

This happens when the helper is more concerned with the problem than with the client. Such people usually have a good technical knowledge of the problem. The helper will obtain as much information as possible and then use his or her expertise to provide a solution. People who often use this style include for example solicitors, accountants and medical professionals.

This approach is quite acceptable as long as (a) the client requires this kind of factual help and (b) the helper has sound, credible knowledge of the problem, and is able to provide the correct solution. The helper is not concerned with the client's learning or personal development and may indeed provide the solution in such a way that, if it occurs again, the client will have to repeat the consultation.

- Tellers use phrases such as, 'Follow these instructions,' 'Do it like this,' 'Call me if it happens again'.

The helper who manipulates

This kind of helper may appear to be more concerned with the client than the problem, but actually excludes the client from the problem-solving process. The helper believes that he knows what is best for the client. He uses undue influence to provide a solution, manipulating the client to accept a solution which will actually satisfy the helper's needs. Users of this style try to make their clients dependent upon them. They tend to have a low opinion of the clients and thus adopt a patronising approach. This is a very dangerous style and you should not let yourself be tempted into it. The style can be recognised by such phrases as 'If I were you . . .', 'Let me help you with that . . .', or 'You seem to have a problem . . .'

The helper who advises

The helper using this style is more concerned with the problem but wants to include the client in the solution whilst still retaining the role of specialist. Such helpers often offer a number of solutions to the client, from which the client is expected to make a choice. These solutions are usually based upon the helper's own experience and may not always be relevant to the present situation. Business consultants often use this approach with their clients. However, people will only accept that advice which agrees with their own thoughts. Advice which is not acceptable is usually countered by the phrase 'Yes but . . .'.

- Typical phrases used by advisers are 'Why don't you . . .', 'My advice to you is . . .', 'What I suggest is . . .'

The helper who counsels

The real counsellor is more concerned with the client than with the problem. The counsellor helps the client to reach his or her own solutions. The counselling style involves more listening than talking. The counsellor uses questions to help the client – not the counsellor – to explore and analyse all aspects of the problem. This style differs from the others in that the helper wants the client to learn as much as possible about the problem solving process in the hope that they will be able to work things out for themselves in the future. Counselling recognises the feelings and emotions that surround a problem.

YOUR ROLE AS COUNSELLOR

As a counsellor your role is twofold:

- firstly to help the client to recognise and accept the real problem
- secondly to help them to reach a solution and to act upon it.

Skills required

The main skills you need as counsellor are:

(a) to be a good, active listener

(b) to encourage the counsellee to talk through the problem

(c) to remain neutral to both the client and the problem.

TYPES OF COUNSELLING

We can broadly divide the different types of counselling into three main groups:

- indirect
- direct
- confrontational.

Indirect counselling

The counsellor has no preconceived ideas about the client, the problem or the solution. The client is encouraged to offer possible solutions, weigh up the pros and cons of each, choose one and act. This is undoubtedly the most effective method in most situations.

Direct counselling

In this case, the counsellor has already decided upon the 'right' solution and manipulates the client towards accepting it. This often happens when the outcome of the solution will affect the counsellor.

Confrontational counselling

This is where the counsellor intentionally provokes the client to make emotionally-based statements about him/herself and other people connected with the problem. This method may be used when the client refuses to admit or recognise the real problem, *eg* alcohol or drug abuse. This method should *only* be employed by highly trained and experienced counsellors.

WHO CAN COUNSEL?

Basically anyone can provide counselling who has acquired the necessary skills, as set out in this book.

The need to remain detached

One of the main difficulties experienced by non-professional counsellors is to remain emotionally uninvolved with the client and/or the problem.

To conduct an effective counselling session, you should begin by knowing as little as possible about your client, so that you are free of any preconceived ideas. It is extremely difficult, if not impossible, to counsel friends and relatives, simply because you know them too well and thus will find it very difficult to distance yourself from the emotional aspect.

Similarly, the last person to counsel an employee should be his or her manager. This is mainly because the manager will have a direct interest in the solution and find it difficult to disassociate him/herself from it. Therefore the counselling tends to be telling or advising.

GOLDEN RULES FOR COUNSELLORS

Do

- Ask questions
- Listen actively
- Observe body language
- Ascertain the core problem
- Be patient
- Remain neutral.

Do not

- Offer solutions
- Give advice
- Be critical or judgemental
- Jump to conclusions
- Show emotion.

Each of these points will be dealt with in detail in succeeding chapters.

POINTS FOR DISCUSSION

1. Have you ever been called upon by colleagues to provide some counselling, even if the word 'counselling' has not been used?

2. How do you think a role as counsellor would help you with your own personal and professional development?

3. Of the four basic styles of helping – telling, manipulating, advising, and counselling – which do you personally feel most/least comfortable with, and why?

2
Identifying the Need for Counselling

In the work environment it is usually left to the immediate manager to initiate a counselling interview. In order to do this, the manager has to identify the particular need for counselling. In many instances, such needs can be obvious – for example persistent lateness, absenteeism, poor quality work, and so on. However, it is also valuable if the manager can identify the possible underlying causes.

Counselling is concerned with 'people problems' and these may be (broadly) divided into three groups:

- personality problems
- work related problems
- external problems.

COUNSELLING FOR PERSONALITY PROBLEMS

Personality problems are related to the image people have of themselves and of others. These images have been classified by American psychologists as 'states of OKness' of which there are four:

I'm OK, you're OK	high image of self and of other people
You're OK, I'm not OK	poor self image and high opinion of others
I'm OK, you're not OK	high image of self but poor opinion of others
I'm not OK, you're not OK	low image of self and of others

Each of the above can be identified by specific behaviours and, with the exception of the first one, can be reasons for counselling.

Typical behaviours

High self image, poor opinion of others

- Aggressive
- Autocratic
- Critical of others but does not accept criticism
- Has very fixed views
- Makes hasty decisions
- Quick tempered
- Enjoys 'points scoring'.

Poor self image, high opinion of others

- Timid
- Anxious to please
- Prefers to help rather than do
- Worries about failure
- Indecisive
- Withdrawn
- Easily influenced by others.

Poor image of self and of others

- Blames others
- Disorganised
- Irrational
- Forgetful
- Defensive
- Paranoid.

Having observed one or more of the above behaviours in a member of his staff, the manager should now have some idea as to how that person perceives himself and his colleagues.

COUNSELLING FOR WORK-RELATED PROBLEMS

Many problems are directly related to job functions and the working environment. A number of these may be a result of how the organisation itself functions; they can only be resolved by making changes to the organisation or by the individual concerned leaving the company.

Key employee concerns

In the 1920s, Professor Mayo of Harvard University was invited by the Western Electric Company of Chicago to supervise a long-term programme of research into the effect of work on human performance. One of the results highlighted the following concerns of employees:

- losing a job
- the job development
- injustices
- poor relations with management
- poor working relationships.

As with personality problems, individual behaviours will reveal many work related problems. Whilst a number of these behaviours are overt and so can be observed, others will become apparent through conversation. Such behaviours and their possible causes include:

Overwork
- Works long hours
- Takes work home
- Everything becomes urgent
- Tiredness
- Irritable and agitated
- Reduced contact with colleagues.

Under employment
- Boredom
- Casual attitude towards work
- Feels frustrated because talents are under used
- Lateness and absenteeism
- Becomes cynical about the company and bosses.

Uncertainty about the future
- Takes on more work to prove ability
- Concerned about promotion
- Reluctant to share information with colleagues
- Constantly seeks reassurance from bosses
- Seeks additional responsibilities.

Inability to cope with technology
– Blames equipment for mistakes
– Regularly refers to the 'good old days'
– Fears making errors
– Poor relationship with technical whizzkids
– Increased absenteeism.

This list is not intended to be complete or unerringly accurate but to offer the manager some clues about the possible causes of behaviours.

COUNSELLING FOR PROBLEMS OUTSIDE WORK

Problems outside work are usually domestic in origin. They may be caused by such events as:

- bereavement
- marriage breakdowns
- family relationships
- serious illnesses
- financial problems.

People suffering such personal problems usually try very hard to keep them hidden at work, believing that the workplace is not the place to discuss them. Yet however hard they try, they will almost certainly exhibit changes in their normal behaviour pattern. These changes should tell the manager that something is wrong.

If the manager has an honest, open, trusting relationship with his/her staff, those with these types of problem may react positively to an invitation to discuss them in confidence. On other occasions, the manager may discover through patient counselling that a personal problem lies at the core.

The counselling of personal problems requires a good deal of specialised skill and experience. As a manager you may feel unable to do anything beyond being empathetic to the client. Again it is very tempting to offer your own solutions but this must be strongly resisted however well meant.

For example, in the case of bereavement of a close relative it would seem natural for a manager to say, 'Why don't you take a few days off?' Whilst some people may accept such an offer, it could be the very opposite of what another individual might need.

By all means offer neutral information, but leave it to the client to accept it or not. If the core problem appears to be a breakdown in marriage, for example, you might well say, 'Relate are experts in dealing with such matters.' Leave it there; don't suggest that the client arranges to see them.

It is more sensible in the case of personal problems simply to provide information rather than attempt to help the client towards a solution; it is unlikely that a manager will be in a position to offer any sound options.

POINTS FOR DISCUSSION

1. You are counselling one of your team members about changes in their behaviour towards their colleagues and have asked a question about the person's family. The other person angrily tells you to mind your own business.

   Would you:

   (a) Immediately apologise and change your line of questioning.

   (b) Ask them why they are so angry.

   (c) Keep quiet and wait for them to say something else.

   (d) Reflect back their feeling.

   (e) Tell them that it is necessary to ask the question in order to discover why they have changed their attitude.

   See page 95 for suggested answers.

2. What key concerns have you yourself experienced as an employee? Did any of these go unrecognised by superiors or colleagues?

3
Communicating Effectively

'What we say is not always what others hear.'

Counselling is all about effective oral and aural communication. As a counsellor you will need to practise a three-step process which is repeated throughout the counselling interview. These three steps are:

- questioning
- listening
- responding.

QUESTIONING

The main reasons for asking questions as a counsellor are:

(a) to relax the client by inviting the client to talk.

(b) to help the client explore the problem and its causes.

(c) to provide the counsellor with relevant information.

Using open questions

The way in which you pose the questions will influence the way they are answered. Since your objective is to get the client to talk, your questions should be framed to encourage this. The simplest method is to ask questions beginning with words such as:

When
Where
What
How
Why

They are usually referred to as **open questions**. Questions that can be answered with a simple yes or no are known as **closed questions**.

Below are a number of closed questions. Re-write each one as an open question, designed to produce more detailed information.

1. Did the interview go well?____________________

2. Do you enjoy the job you are doing?____________________

3. Are you getting on OK with your work colleagues?____________

4. Do you have a good social life?____________________

5. Do you find the work difficult?____________________

See page 95 for suggested answers.

USING DIFFERENT TYPES OF QUESTION

Taking this a stage further, you can use different types of questions to guide your client towards providing specific information:

- elaboration questions
- specific questions
- feelings questions
- behavioural questions
- opinion questions.

Asking for elaboration

These give the client the opportunity to talk freely and can provide the counsellor with valuable clues. It is a good method of opening the interview.

Examples
'Tell me about . . . '
'Describe . . . '

Asking specific questions

These ask the client to provide specific information, often about points raised during the answer to the elaboration.

Examples
'When did this happen?'
'How long ago was that?'

Asking about feelings

These investigate how the client felt at certain times or after particular events.

Examples
'How did you feel when . . .?'
'What did you feel about . . .?'

Asking what the client did

These discover how the client reacted to specific events. The way in which a person behaved in the past is a guide to how they will react in the future to similar happenings.

Examples
'What did you do when . . .?'
'And after that?'

Asking the client's opinion

Most people like to be asked and to give their opinions. Apart from revealing the client's views, it can also be useful in moving the interview along should the client be hesitant in answering other questions, as it should be seen as non-threatening.

Examples
'What do you think about . . .?'
'What are your views on . . .?'

QUESTIONS TO AVOID

As a counsellor you should avoid asking the following types of questions.

Leading questions

Example: 'You would agree with me that . . . wouldn't you?' This will be seen by the client as coercive. The client is likely to become defensive.

Multi-choice questions

For example, 'Would you prefer to do . . . or . .?' Faced with such a question, the client may feel backed into a corner and become tense.

Multiple questions

This means asking several questions together without waiting for an answer. The client will generally answer the easiest question only.

Since questions are the main tool of the counsellor, they need to be used carefully. Some questions can be planned before the interview, but others will come about as a result of listening to the answers.

LISTENING TO THE CLIENT

Listening is a key skill and one that other people value and respect. Those who can demonstrate this skill will soon find that people will come to them just to have them listen.

Hearing is not listening

Hearing is	*Listening is*
An aural impulse	A mental process
Physiological	Intellectual
Awareness (of a verbal message)	Understanding (of the meaning of a verbal message)
An inherent quality	An acquired skill

Active listening

'Active listening' is a phrase coined by Carl Rogers. It means *demonstrating* to the speaker that you are listening to what is being said. This skill is vital to any counsellor and must be practised as it does not always come naturally. The following techniques will help you to acquire this skill.

Maintaining eye contact

Looking at the speaker will show them that you are listening. This does not mean staring them straight in the eye, as they may find that threatening.

Continuation behaviour

This is achieved by nodding your head and using encouraging noises such as 'Uh-huh'. Such behaviour will help the speaker to continue to talk in the knowledge that you are listening to them.

Tolerating pauses
When the speaker pauses, do not be tempted to jump in with a question or comment. Give the other person time to gather their thoughts and continue.

Reflecting facts
Repeat the last word or phrase of the speaker, to show you are following them.

Reflecting feelings
You need to judge the emotion behind what the speaker says and reflect it back. For example, 'You feel unhappy about that.' It is important to identify the right emotion, otherwise the speaker may feel cheated and that you have not listened properly. If someone is obviously angry about something and you reflect back disappointment, rather than empathy, your credibility as a good listener will be diminished.

Summarising
This simply means repeating a condensed version of what has been said.

Using body language
Ensure that you are using the appropriate body language. This will be covered in more detail on page 26.

Remaining neutral
Refrain from showing emotion either at what is being said or about the person themselves. You may not like the other person's appearance, attitude or behaviour but a good listener will not let this affect their active listening skills.

Summary
The importance of good listening cannot be over-emphasised. It is the key skill for a counsellor.

CASE STUDY

Reflect back the following statements:

(a) I'm always ignored when it comes to promotion.

(b) The work is boring.
(c) Nobody ever listens to my ideas.
(d) Everyone always seems to be having a go at me.
(e) There are no prospects in this company any more.
(f) The company only thinks about cutting costs, never about the people.

For suggested answers turn to page 95.

RESPONDING TO THE CLIENT

How we respond to what has been said will indicate how well we have listened. The success or otherwise of a counselling interview will often depend upon the type of responses that we give.

At the end of this chapter (pages 28 to 42) is a counselling style assessment for you to complete which will illustrate your preferred method of responding. It will indicate what, if any, changes you need to make to become a successful counsellor.

NON VERBAL COMMUNICATION

Non verbal communication – more commonly referred to as **body language** – is a very important part of any face-to-face communication. Unlike words or tone of voice, both of which can communicate the speaker's feelings, body language is extremely difficult for anyone to control for more than a few moments at a time. Because our movements and gestures are subconscious, they will exhibit our true feelings, even though we may carefully choose the words and control our tone.

Much research has been carried out and numerous books written about body language. The main points to consider are:

(a) Clusters – the existence of two or more postures that may indicate the person's feelings.

(b) Changes – when a person alters posture in response to a question or statement.

The counsellor's posture

The counsellor should adopt the appropriate posture, that is one that is open and confident. This can best be achieved by sitting with both feet flat on the floor, or cross legged if this is more comfortable. The hands should be placed palm down on the thighs. There should be no physical barrier such as a desk or table between the counsellor and the client. You are recommended not to take notes during the interview as this can make the client alarmed or suspicious.

The client's posture

The counsellor should observe the posture of the client, particularly any changes of posture. For example, if after having been asked a question, the client folds his arms and crosses his legs, this may indicate that he feels defensive about the question.

Typical postures

Here is a brief list of postures and their possible meanings:

- Clenched hands, leaning forward slightly – apprehensive, worried.
- Fingering the collar – may not be telling the whole truth.
- Stroking chin – considering what has been said.
- Pulling earlobe – the person wants to speak.
- Scratching neck – doubt or uncertainty.
- Hand over mouth – may be telling lies.
- Rubbing nose – negative thoughts.
- Chin on palm with fingers in or near mouth – seeking reassurance.
- Tapping fingers – irritated.
- Tapping feet – had enough and wants to leave.

These are *only* indicators, however, and must be viewed with some caution.

While a client remains in a defensive posture his or her thoughts and feelings will be defensive and this will not aid the progress of the interview. One technique that the counsellor can use to try and change the client's attitude is to mirror the client's posture and after a few moments, move back to an open posture; there is a good chance that the client will do likewise.

ASSESSING STYLES OF COMMUNICATION RESPONSE

This assessment exercise contains a series of twenty statements made by imaginary persons. Following each statement are four possible responses. Your job is to select the response(s) that you most agree with . . . the one(s) you would be likely to make if you were responding to that person face-to-face.

For each of the twenty statements you have three points to assign, giving them to one or more of the responses. Here's what a typical statement and its four responses look like:

Example

'One of my newer employees seems more interested in her own needs than she is in working on departmental goals and standards.'

A Why do you think she is putting her own needs ahead of the organisation's?

B Maybe you haven't spent enough time communicating your department's goals and standards.

C I think you should tell your employee how you feel and at the same time get her to express her views on the situation.

D It must be very difficult for you to supervise such a person.

How to score your answers

For ease of scoring we suggest you write the value you are assigning to a statement to the right of the letter and before the statement.

To summarise. You must assign three points to each set of four statements, you can assign the points any way you like *ie* give one statement all 3 points, split the points giving one statement 1 point and another 2 points or, give three statements 1 point each.

Do not dwell on any set of statements too long, there are no right and wrong answers and no trick questions. The result of this assignment will be an interpretation of your preferred communication response style.

❑ **Group One**

'I think I'm doing all right but I don't know where I stand. I'm not sure what my boss expects of me and he doesn't tell me how I'm doing. I'm trying my best, but I wonder who else knows that. I wish I knew where I stood.'

A Not knowing if you're satisfying your boss or not is like being in the middle of nowhere.

B If you gave it a little thought, you'd realise that feedback from your boss isn't always a good thing.

C Has your boss ever given you any indication of what he thinks about your work?

❑ **Group Two**

'It happens every time the manager appears in my department. She just takes over. She orders my people around as if I wasn't there. When she sees something she doesn't like, she tells them what to do and how to do it. They get confused. I get upset and then finally she leaves. I'm responsible to her, so what can I do?'

A You're not sure what would be the most appropriate way to confront your manager about your feelings regarding her behaviour.

B It sounds to me that you're getting more upset than your people are.

C How long has this been going on?

D You should discuss the problem with the boss.

❑ **Group Three**

'I finally feel I'm on board with the rest of my sales group. I got a big sale from one of my key accounts that pushed me over my sales quota. For only being on the job nine months I feel good about my progress.'

A How much over quota are you?

B You should work out what it was you did to land that big sale so you can repeat this success story.

C Sounds exciting! Hitting your sales quota in such a short time must give you a feeling of satisfaction.

D Are you sure you're doing as well as you think you are? Maybe others have reached their quota in four to six months.

Fig. 3. Communication response style – assessment exercise.

❑ Group Four

'As long as I've got a goal ahead, I'll keep striving for it. I'm determined to advance; hard work never bothered me. I know it won't be easy and I'll probably have to climb over a few people to get my way. This is important to me; I want to be somebody and I will be.'

A Can you imagine how you would feel if other people treated you in this way?

B What in particular do you wish to achieve?

C You should take some classes in management to help you speed up your advancement.

D I can see that getting ahead in your life is very important even if it means hard work and climbing over others.

❑ Group Five

'I've worked here for a long time but I still don't know anybody. I try to take an interest in the people I work with, but I just can't seem to make friends. I feel uncomfortable and just seem to freeze up. Sometimes I try to pretend that I don't want friends because people can be a lot of trouble at times – everyone trying to do better than the next. Sometimes I think I really believe that.'

A Why do you think you have difficulty making friends?

B Many people have this kind of problem but I think it might be a good idea to be more friendly and talk more to people you meet.

C It sounds like you don't make friends easily because you clam up and feel unsure of yourself.

D You have got to give a little you know.

❑ Group Six

'The company policy is supposed to be to hire from within.I now find this new person is coming in to take the place of my boss. I had my eyes on that job; I've been working hard for it. I know I could do the job – I could prove myself if I have a chance. Well if that's what they think of me, I know when I am not wanted.'

A Maybe your qualifications don't compare with those of the new person.

B Did they discuss it with you at all?

Fig. 3. Assessment exercise (continued).

C I would make sure they know your views and let them know your interest in advancement.

D It's annoying when the company seems to have forgotten about you; hiring from outside the company when you put a lot of hard work into your job.

❑ Group Seven

'I had one of the most difficult customers to deal with yesterday. Not once did I let my emotions take control of me. I kept to the issues, listened with understanding and examined alternatives with the customer until she found one that would work best for her. The customer was satisfied and even told me that I handled the situation very well.'

A What kind of problem did the customer have?

B Sounds like you feel proud of the way you were able to handle a difficult customer in a calm way plus come up with a workable solution.

C You should follow that procedure every time you have a difficult customer to deal with.

D You shouldn't let a customer tell you what solution is the best one.

❑ Group Eight

'It all boils down to the fact that I'm in the wrong job. I've hesitated about leaving for a long time because I spent years in college preparing myself for this type of work. Now I think I would be much happier if I leave this job behind and enter another field – even though I'll be starting at the bottom of the ladder.'

A You really should stay in the job you have since you don't know what you might be getting into if you change jobs.

B To change jobs after spending years at college to prepare for your profession is a big decision – one that's not going to be easy for you to make.

C Do you think you should give up your years at college just like that?

D What is it that might appeal to you about another job?

❑ Group Nine

'She used to be one of the gang. Then she was promoted. She's not my friend anymore. I don't mind being told about my mistakes but she

Fig. 3. Assessment exercise (continued).

doesn't have to do it in front of my work mates. Whenever I get a chance she's going to get hers.'

A You shouldn't waste your energy trying to get even with her.

B To be told about your mistakes in front of colleagues is embarrassing especially by a supervisor you once used to work with.

C How often has she done this?

D Why don't you talk it over with a few people who knew her before and then go talk to her about this situation?

❑ Group Ten

'I'm really tired of this. I come in the morning and already I've got twice as much work as I can do that day. And then they say that 'this is a rush', or 'hurry up on that'. I've got so many people asking me to do things that I just can't keep up, and that bothers me. I like my boss and my work is interesting but I sure could use a vacation.'

A Is responding to all these requests from other people part of your job?

B You seem to have too much work. Why not talk it over with your boss?

C With so many people asking you to do things it's difficult for you to get everything done and the pressure is getting you down.

D You're probably overworked because you're not organised.

❑ Group Eleven

'The sales department gets all the money and attention. We produce 100,000 of these a day and we don't even have enough money to replace these old machines. It's a tough job, but we do it. The sales people get all the glory and we make as big a contribution as they do. What do we have to show for our efforts? – Nothing.'

A You should talk to the other department heads about this.

B When you put a great deal of effort into a job and don't get credit, you feel let down and annoyed.

C You're probably not giving the others in sales enough credit for the job they're doing.

D In particular, what do they get that you would like to have?

Fig. 3. Assessment exercise (continued).

❑ **Group Twelve**

'If only I had enough money I would jump at the opportunity. I'm sure I could make a go of that business. All it needs is a little vision, some common sense, and the courage to try it, and I've got all three. I just don't have the money to do it. That's life, I guess.'

A Are you sure you could make a go of a business on your own?

B What kind of business do you have in mind?

C What you should do is discuss it with a banker – one that specialises in starting new business.

D It's disappointing not to have the money you need to get into a business you feel you'd make a success of.

❑ **Group Thirteen**

'During my monthly work planning meeting with my boss, I brought up a suggestion for reducing the paperwork. It's an idea I've had for some time. It took me six hours to work it out and get it down on paper. My boss quickly saw how my idea could save time and money and wants me to work with Bob to put it into effect next week.'

A Are you sure it's an idea that will really work?

B If I were you, I'd make sure that your boss tells Bob that it's a good idea.

C Having an idea accepted so readily by your boss gives you a feeling of worth and importance.

D How long did it take to develop your idea?

❑ **Group Fourteen**

'I don't know what I'm going to do. I'm making all kinds of mistakes and I know my supervisor is unhappy with me. She's already yelled at me twice this week. I can't stand being yelled at.'

A Why do you think you're making so many mistakes?

B Why don't you tell your supervisor how you feel?

C It's disturbing to have someone yell at you when you make mistakes.

D Perhaps your supervisor has good reason to yell at you.

❑ **Group Fifteen**

'Oh brother! A person in our department got a promotion by buttering

Fig. 3. Assessment exercise (continued).

up the higher ups! That promotion should have been mine. I think I am more qualified than he is. He doesn't need the money half as much as I do.'

A If I were you I'd tell your manager how angry you're feeling.

B It's disappointing to have someone get a promotion you were counting on.

C It seems to me you haven't done your job as well as you think you have or you would have got the promotion yourself.

D Has this happened to you before?

❏ Group Sixteen

'My supervisor often makes mistakes and has me handle the situation for her. It ends up that she avoids confronting the issue directly. To add insult to injury she says to me, "It's your fault, you should watch out for those mistakes!"

A I wouldn't let anybody treat me that way.

B It seems to me you're caught in a no-win situation and resent being treated this way.

C What kind of mistakes does she ask you to cover up?

D You should ask for a transfer and find a job where you're treated fairly.

❏ Group Seventeen

'It's happened again! I was describing an office problem to my boss when he started staring out of the window. He doesn't seem to be really listening to me because he has to ask me to repeat things to him. I feel he's superficially giving me the time to state my problems but he ends up side-stepping the issues.'

A You should stop talking when you feel he's not listening to you. That way he'll start paying attention to you.

B You can't expect him to listen to every problem you have . . . you should learn to solve your own problems.

C What kind of problems do you talk to him about?

D It's frustrating to have your boss behave in this way when you're talking about problems that are important for you to solve.

Fig. 3. Assessment exercise (continued).

❑ **Group Eighteen**

'I received a performance review last week. It's the best one I've ever received. I've been working on communicating more clearly to my co-workers and following instructions more carefully. I guess I'm listening better to instructions . . . none of my paperwork has to be done again. My boss also mentioned I was fostering group cohesiveness and showing consideration for other people's needs.'

A When did you start working to improve your communication skills?

B You should get a copy of your appraisal and keep it for future reference.

C I remember last week you had to redo the planning project because you had some wrong totals typed in.

D You should really pleased that the hard work you did to improve your communication skills paid off with such positive results.

❑ **Group Nineteen**

'I work like mad to get rush projects completed! What's my reward for getting them out? Nothing! No thanks, no nothing. In fact, most of the time the so called rush projects sit on people's desks unattended for days.'

A How often does this happen?

B You ought to tell them that you don't like being treated unfairly.

C It appears to me you feel like they're taking advantage of you, and that you're being treated unfairly.

D You shouldn't get so angry.

❑ **Group Twenty**

'I don't know what I'm going to go. My boss keeps asking me to work overtime, to get letters out or finish a project that could wait until the next day. I can't say anything because he's my boss. I'd sure like to tell him a thing or two, but I just can't risk it.'

A Sounds like you feel you're being taken advantage of and want to find a way to confront your boss about his behaviour.

B If I were you, I'd discuss it with him. You should tell him how you feel.

C If you didn't act like such a doormat, you would have stood up to him by now.

D Has your boss always treated you this way?

Fig. 3. Assessment exercise (continued).

Communication response style – answer sheet

1		5		9		13		17	
A	*	A	O	A	+	A	+	A	=
B	+	B	=	B	*	B	=	B	+
C	O	C	*	C	O	C	*	C	O
D	=	D	+	D	=	D	O	D	*

2		6		10		14		18	
A	*	A	+	A	O	A	O	A	O
B	+	B	O	B	=	B	=	B	=
C	O	C	=	C	*	C	*	C	+
D	=	D	*	D	+	D	+	D	*

3		7		11		15		19	
A	O	A	O	A	=	A	=	A	O
B	=	B	*	B	*	B	*	B	=
C	*	C	=	C	+	C	+	C	*
D	+	D	+	D	O	D	O	D	+

4		8		12		16		20	
A	+	A	=	A	+	A	+	A	*
B	O	B	*	B	O	B	*	B	=
C	=	C	+	C	=	C	O	C	+
D	*	D	O	D	*	D	=	D	O

Transfer the points you have allocated when you considered your response to the 20 groups, write the points after the letter in each of ther 20 boxes above. When you have completed that step add up the total for each symbol [* = + O] and write it against the symbol in the diagram on page 37.

Communication response style: symbols, scores & meaning

Symbol		Total
*	Empathetic	
+	Critical	
O	Searching	
=	Advising	

Comment

The highest total indicates the response style with which you feel most comfortable even though it may not be the most suitable. Read the interpretation on the following pages to see the likely effect of using each style.

COMMUNICATION RESPONSE STYLE INTERPRETATION

The need for awareness

A vital ingredient of effective communication is being aware of the power you have to affect how the other person(s) will respond to you. The more effectively you listen and respond to others, the more they become aware – even subconsciously – of your responsiveness. As a result, they are more likely to respond positively when your turn comes to talk. In short, your response style serves as a model for those you communicate with, and it is likely to influence their response style when it's their turn to listen.

If we want to be effective in our dealings with others, it's important to know the kinds of things we do that cause distrust and misunderstanding. Ever hear complaints such as: 'I'd like to help Peter, but he won't listen to anything I say.' Or perhaps you've heard: 'I want to help but people get defensive when I give advice.' Or maybe you've heard this one: 'Why do they all go to Janet to discuss their problems? I'm their supervisor . . . not her.' By developing an awareness of our response patterns, by knowing the behaviours we use that turn people off or that influence them to feel understood, we can expand our ability to influence others positively.

Below and in the following pages a description of the four response styles can be found. All four were present in each of the groups in the assessment, and you already have your four scores to reflect the strength of each style. Here is what each score means.

Empathetic response

A non-judgemental reply that captures the essential theme and/or feeling expressed. This communication mode reflects a positive attitude, sorts out elements of personal value, and goes all the way in making the communication a two-way exchange. A person in this mode will listen between the lines for underlying meanings, will keep an open mind by staying out of a judgmental framework, and will focus on what would be useful to do rather than on what is wrong. This person concentrates on fostering respect, rapport, trust and understanding.

By holding back on our rebuttals, we can keep a more objective point of view. The empathic response stimulates the other person by being attentive, alert, and interested in their needs. Such responses encourage the other person to elaborate on their ideas and feelings. They will be willing to open up to the degree that we remain non-judgmental and non-critical. The empathic listener is like a mirror, reflecting what the other person is feeling. This leads people to open up, comfortable in the assurance that they can talk openly without being criticised or judged.

A major element of this communication style is that the empathic responder avoids the temptation to give advice. When people are given the opportunity to talk about and talk through their problems, they have a better understanding of the implications of their problem and will be able to work out their own action plan. Although empathic responders avoid suggesting a solution, they can still remain a resource person who can share information when appropriate. It is important to remember that you don't have to agree with what a person is saying to be an empathic listener. Your empathy extends to their feelings and what they might be experiencing... it need not extend to their actions.

Critical response

The critical response expresses judgment or evaluation that the other person often perceives as a put-down. This response often results from our natural tendency to judge others, either approvingly or disapprovingly. This responding style often challenges what people say and why they feel the way they do. Even though people may tell you that they want feedback and evaluation, most people do not take kindly to criticism, regardless of the spirit in which it was given. Indeed, as Mark Twain once wrote, 'there is no such thing as constructive criticism'.

Because a critical response is often perceived as a threat, it increases the emotional level of the other person who feels turned off, labelled and categorised, and thus may choose not to respond. When we become critical, we are likely to 'get hooked' into negative feelings that will cloud our objectivity and cause us to jump to false or premature conclusions.

Many factors can lead us to make critical responses. One is the pressure of time and conflicting priorities (*ie* we have other things to do beside listen to that other person's problems). Another is that the values and ideas of the other person may differ from our own, thus biasing us. Still another is that we have our own experiences and needs, and in our desire to share these with others, we inadvertently adopt ways that are easily construed as being critical or judgmental.

There are three unfortunate outcomes of the critical response:

(1) the other person feels rejected or put down

(2) they will usually retreat or 'clam up'.

(3) they will not have a chance to release the feelings and emotions that may be begging for expression. We all give way to critical responses from time to time. What is important is that we know when it's happening and work to overcome the problems that our critical responses may create.

Search response

The searching response asks for additional information. Sometimes we need more facts and feelings so as to understand the other person.

Sometimes the additional information will help us to get to the root of a problem. Sometimes we want to help the other person to 'ventilate' and thereby express their emotions. These are good reasons for using a searching response.

But there are times when a searching response is inappropriate. Too many questions can be felt as interrogation . . . a feeling of being 'grilled' or given the 'third degree'. Then too, we sometimes ask questions to fulfil our own needs and not out of concern for the other person. This may disrupt their train of thought. At times we are so busy thinking up our next question that we fail to listen to the other person's response to our last question.

The timing of our searching response is very important. For example, consider the person who is speaking emotionally and in fragmented sentences, describing a current experience – something dear to them that was just stolen. Even though we have a lot of questions to ask, we might want to use a few empathic ones first ("Sounds like you're at a real loss" . . . "You must feel awful, having lost a family heirloom.") to get their emotional level down to the point where they can think objectively and talk coherently. Then, when you feel they can be logical and analytical, you are ready to use the searching response.

Advising response

The advising response is a recommendation that tells the other person what to do or not do. When we are busy thinking of solutions while the other person is talking, we cannot listen fully to what they are saying.

There's a common myth that many people perpetuate: the notion that when someone comes to us with a problem, it's our job to solve it . . . or at least tell them what to do. Even when people report on something they've done (successfully or unsuccessfully), we feel obliged to tell them what to do next.

When we give another person advice, we deprive them of the chance to talk through the problem or opportunity. This kind of communication mode tends to build dependency relationships. The best help we can give others is to enable them to work out their own solutions. People feel more self confident and behave more maturely (independently) when they can plan and organise their own situations rather than have others tell them what to do.

Sometimes we give advice out of a genuine desire to help. Sometimes our recommendations are prompted by our own ego needs

– for status, prestige, power etc. But whatever our motivation, advice is usually given at the expense of the other person's personal and professional development. It's OK to supply information, ideas and facts, but we hinder others when we give them advice on things they need to work out for themselves.

Personal interpretation and plan of action

My most frequent response is the________________ response.

My next most frequent style is the________________ response.

My third most frequent style is the________________ response.

My least frequent style is the________________ response.

Based on the order of responses noted above, I would conclude that my communication response style might best be described as:

____

____

____

____

The implication of my response style is that in my communication with others I will have to make a conscious effort to:________________

____

____

____

____

I will know that I've been successful when the other person I'm communicating with begins to:________________________

____

____

____

____

____

POINTS FOR DISCUSSION

1. You have received a complaint from another manager about the behaviour of one of your staff. What action would you take?

    (a) Ignore it.

    (b) Arrange to counsel the staff member about his/her behaviour.

    (c) Obtain as many facts as possible about the incident.

    (d) Counsel the manager.

    (e) Warn your member of staff to improve their behaviour in future.

    For suggested answers see page 95.

2. How could you make your own personal communication more effective?

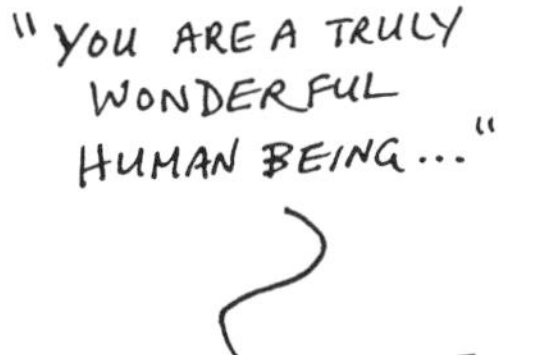

4
Managing the Counselling Interview

In the case of the professional counsellor, the client will have been aware of a problem and requested the interview. The client is thus prepared for counselling even though he or she may not know what is involved or how things will proceed. In the workplace, the manager has ideally developed a sufficiently good and trusting relationship with his/her staff, that staff members will approach the manager to discuss their problems. However, with time constraints and work pressures, this rarely happens. Therefore as a good manager it is up to you to initiate counselling with your staff.

SETTING UP THE INTERVIEW

The first step is for you to recognise the need for counselling. This is not easy as most people tend to conceal their personal problems, particularly whilst at work. They fear that to reveal them will be taken as a sign of weakness by colleagues and bosses.

As a manager, it is an important part of your job to observe each and every member of your team and to spot any unexplained changes in behaviour or performance. It is not too difficult to detect behavioural changes as when a normally happy and cooperative person becomes quiet and uncommunicative or noisy and disruptive. There will be a reason for such a change in behaviour. Similarly, why does someone who is usually accurate and careful with their work suddenly become sloppy and careless? It may well be a 'cry for help'. People subconsciously wanting help may instinctively draw attention to themselves. Whereas they may not feel able to approach others with their problems, they are giving out signals asking for someone to say, 'What is the problem? Can I help?' Although they may initially reject such approaches, they will know and feel inwardly reassured that help is available.

Creating the right interview opportunity

Once you have determined the need for counselling, the next step is to create the right opportunity for it. This requires planning, which should include:

- setting aside 30 minutes to an hour for the interview
- ensuring complete privacy with no interruptions
- creating a comfortable environment – this can be achieved by getting rid of all physical barriers such as desks and arranging the seats at right angles to each other.
- providing a credible reason for meeting, such as to discuss a project, sales figures, training and so on.

STARTING THE INTERVIEW

Your aim should be to conduct the meeting in an open, friendly and non-critical manner, beginning with its original purpose (*eg* to discuss a project). This will help to create the right atmosphere for what is to follow.

Example

Let us assume that the reason you wish to counsel this particular employee (Tom) is because he has become less punctual lately and leaves the office promptly at the end of the day; until recently Tom would have completed his tasks before leaving.

You can begin the counselling with a statement such as:

'I've noticed that you are not quite as punctual in the mornings as you used to be.'

Leave the statement hanging and wait for a response. How you continue will depend upon the reply. For example:

(a) *Tom*: 'Yes I know. I'm sorry about that.'
You: 'OK, fine, but what's the reason?'

(b) *Tom*: 'Have I?'
You: 'Yes.' (Keep quiet and wait for Tom to continue.)

(c) *Tom*: 'So what?'
You: 'Well, it's causing me a problem when people ask for you and I don't know where you are. What is the reason?'

ENCOURAGING PEOPLE TO TALK

Because of the difference in status between you and your employee, the employee may be reluctant to talk. Experience may have taught him or her to be cautious and not admit any inadequacies to bosses. Therefore the onus is on you as the counsellor to encourage the person to talk. The following techniques can help to achieve this:

1. Remain positive, open and calm, both in voice and in posture.

2. Ask open questions that will help the counsellee to talk.

3. Offer positive reassurance so that the counsellee really knows that you wish to be helpful, not critical nor judgemental. For example, say: 'That must be difficult.' Or, 'I appreciate the problem.'

4. Listen actively; give the speaker your full attention.

5. Reflect and summarise what is being said.

REACHING THE CORE PROBLEM

Once the interview reaches the stage of exploring the underlying cause of the client's change of behaviour, attitude and so on, the client may well initially give a surface or **presenting** problem (a problem which appears simple to solve).

Example

For example, if the client is making uncharacteristic errors at work, they may give reasons such as (a) the work is repetitive and unchallenging, (b) they are bored, or (c) tiredness. If the counsellor tries to help the client to solve these presenting problems at face value, any improvement in performance will only be short lived.

Your long term aim

Behind every presenting problem is a real cause or 'core' problem and it is only when this is revealed and dealt with that there will be any long term improvements. It is the task of the counsellor to expose the core problem. It is not easy and requires a great deal of questioning, listening and patience. Asking about feelings and behaviour can be very helpful (see page 48).

Discovering 'when' and 'what'

A valuable technique is to determine *when* any changes in behaviour etc took place and *what* if anything happened to the client at that time which may have caused such changes.

Example

Suppose the presenting problem is tiredness; the dialogue may proceed along the following lines:

Client: I just feel very tired these days.
Counsellor: When did you start to feel like this?
Client: About six months ago.
Counsellor: I see. What changes in your life happened six months ago?
Client: Nothing really.
Counsellor: Nothing (*silence*).
Client: I did start to learn French at evening class.
Counsellor: Is this for a qualification?
Client: Yes, GCSE.
Counsellor: How many evenings does this take each week?
Client: Two.
Counsellor: How much homework do you have?
Client: More than I expected. It takes up another evening.
Counsellor: Do you enjoy it?
Client: At first, but now it has become a bit of a chore.
Counsellor: What made you decide to learn French?
Client: My father said it would be a good idea, what with the European Union and so on.
Counsellor: Do you live with your parents?
Client: Yes, but I hope to move away soon.

The counsellor may pursue this line of questioning to discover if the client feels pressurised by the father. That may be the core problem. However, one must never jump to conclusions; continue to obtain as many facts as possible.

This is often the most sensitive part of any counselling interview and needs to be handled with care. Ensure that the person does not feel threatened by your questions. If you sense that they are, turn away and change your tack. It may take two or more sessions to discover the core problem, for the client will only reveal it when they feel comfortable with you and you have won their trust. And remember, the client may not realise the real cause of the aberrant behaviour.

In summary

- Recognise the presenting problem.
- Do not attempt to solve these problems.
- Ask questions, particularly feelings and behavioural ones, to get behind the presenting problem.
- Listen carefully and actively to the answers.
- Use the time technique where appropriate.
- Never make assumptions or jump to conclusions.

EXPLORING FEELINGS

Having discovered the core problem, your next task as counsellor is to explore the client's feelings about the problem. This is achieved by asking 'feelings' questions such as:

'How did you feel when . . .?'

'What did you feel about that?'

The answers will provide valuable clues. Remember, the tone of the client's voice will tend to reveal the true feelings.

Example

Counsellor: How did you feel when your father suggested that you learned French?

Client: (a) Fine, I thought it was a good idea.

or

(b) Alright, I suppose, but I didn't really want to spend my evenings in a classroom.

With the first response, there does not appear to be any initial resentment towards the father. However, the second response showed some reluctance to agree and possibly only to please the father. It is very important to bring these feelings into the open and to get the client to recognise their existence. The feelings will affect how the client approaches a solution to the problem.

SOLVING THE UNDERLYING PROBLEM

The client's responsibility

Having discovered the real problem and the feelings involved, it is *not* the role of the counsellor to solve it. In fact one should *never* try to do so, however tempting it may be. Most manager-counsellors find this very difficult; after all, they are trained to find solutions as part of their managerial role.

- The important point to remember is that **the counsellee owns the problem**: it is up to the counsellee to solve it.

Counselling is all about:

– helping people to accept *responsibility* for their problem
– assisting them to work out *their own* solutions.

Once a problem has been recognised and accepted, the counsellor needs to ask the client how they themselves could solve it. Help them to talk through each possible solution to think about the likely consequences; to choose the most acceptable and action it.

The counsellor's contribution

During this process, the counsellor needs to be empathetic, friendly and neutral. Again this proves difficult for many manager-counsellors as the solution most acceptable to the client may not suit the counsellor from a management point of view. Nevertheless, even if you believe that the chosen course will not work, you must allow the client to try it.

Techniques to aid the counsellor at this point in the interview include:

Ask the counsellee for his/her ideas.
'How could you improve the situation?'

'What do you think the options are?'
'What ideas do you have?'

Admit your own fallibility.
'I would feel tired after training four evenings a week.'
'I would find that difficult, too.'
'I must admit, I've often made that mistake.'

Question the options.
'So what would happen if you tried that?'
'How would that help you?'
'How would your colleagues feel about that?'

Being asked for a solution

There will be times when a client is unable to offer any solutions and will ask you for one. In such cases, offer relevant information but do not express your views or make suggestions as to a specific solution.

Examples

(a) 'Why don't you find out if the company will sponsor you?' – *Wrong*.
'The company operates various sponsorship schemes.' – *Right*.

(b) 'I suggest you ask if there is anyone who works here and lives near you so that you can get a lift in the mornings.' – *Wrong*.
'A number of people here have arranged a car-sharing system.' – *Right*.

(c) 'Go and see Peter Davis in the Personnel Department.' – *Wrong*.
'Peter Davis in the Personnel Department has been able to help other people in similar circumstances.' – *Right*.

In the above *Right* examples, it is left to the client to make the next move if he or she wishes.

Should you feel that you have to make suggestions, offer them as tentative questions or statements.

'Have you considered . . ?'

'One option may be . . .'

'I believe that the local library has information about . . .'

Whilst not personalising the situation by stating what you would or have done, it is quite acceptable to give 'third party' information.

> 'Why don't you have a word with Daphne Green in Accounts? She had a similar problem.' – *Wrong.*
>
> 'I understand that Daphne Green in Accounts had a similar problem and she went to the Citizens Advice Bureau who were able to help her.' – *Right.*

There will be times when the problem will require professional guidance. Whilst you may know that this is the only answer, only provide neutral information.

> 'I suggest you arrange to see a Relate counsellor.' – *Wrong.*
> 'Relate are experts in these situations.' – *Right.*

Continuing the example contained in the previous section, let us assume that the client has accepted that the real reason for her changed behaviour is tiredness due to her evening classes.

Counsellor:	From our discussion, it would appear that the evening classes are causing you to feel tired during the day, is that right?
Client:	Yes that's right and it's certainly affecting my work.
Counsellor:	What suggestions do you have to overcome this?
Client:	I could give up the evening classes.
Counsellor:	Yes, you could. How would your parents feel about that?
Client:	They'd obviously be very disappointed.
Counsellor:	I see. How would you feel about that?
Client:	Well, they have always been very good to me, so I don't want to let them down.
Counsellor:	What other options are there?
Client:	I really don't know. What would you suggest?
Counsellor:	A couple of years ago, a friend of mine learned Conversational French. It only took up one evening a week and there was virtually no homework.
Client:	That's a good idea. I'll look into that.

CASE STUDY

You have started a counselling session with one of your staff. Both of you have agreed for the meeting to take place. The need to meet has arisen due to a continued downturn in work performance. You have a room set aside and have taken steps to ensure that you are not disturbed for the next two hours.

You have put a lot of thought into the meeting and have made every effort to get it off to a good start.

Five minutes into the meeting you are still going through the preliminaries. Discussion has not even begun on the subject of reduced performance when it becomes obvious that your staff member is beginning to lose his/her composure. With increasing concern you believe that he/she is going to break down completely unless you do something about it.

Which of the following actions might you take?

(a) Tell the person that you are aware this could be difficult but they have nothing to worry about.

(b) Leave the room to get you both a cup of tea or coffee.

(c) Suggest that they pull themselves together as their behaviour does not help anything.

(d) Offer to adjourn the meeting and arrange a future date.

(e) Tell the person that you are not finding it easy either but you both need to talk through the matter of work performance.

(f) Reflect back the feeling that you have observed and wait for them to reply.

(g) Talk about the weather, last night's television or some other non-relevant topic to take their mind off whatever is worrying them.

See p96 for suggested answers.

5
How to Control the Emotion

RELATIONSHIPS AND FEELINGS

Counselling is to do with how people communicate and behave towards one another. Ideally this relationship within counselling will be characterised by such words as 'trust', 'encouragement', 'honesty' and 'confidentiality'. Unfortunately the ways in which people feel about each other, or the subject of the counselling, get in the way. This is particularly so when the counselling is between a manager and subordinate, when the pressures of work and the different status of those involved are often paramount.

WHEN CHANGE MEANS PAIN

People behave differently in different situations. Someone normally considered calm and rational may experience a problem which makes them angry and very emotional. Because counselling is about helping the *client* to reach a solution to a problem, it usually requires the client to change his or her feelings and attitudes towards the problem. This can be a very emotional process. The counsellor needs to analyse the client's initial feelings from what they say and how they say it.

A method of analysing human behaviour was developed by the late Eric Berne, an American psychologist. This is known as **transactional analysis.**

Before reading further, it is suggested that you complete the questionnaire on pages 54 to 57. This will help you to answer the questions without being influenced by the subsequent explanation of transactional analysis.

TRANSACTIONAL ANALYSIS
Profiles
Part 1

Instructions

If you agree more than you disagree with a statement, mark a plus (+).

If you disagree more than you agree, mark a minus (-). There is no time limit. However, your answers should be spontaneous.

( ) 1. Teenagers would be better off if they tried harder to understand and utilise the experience of older persons.

( ) 2. I enjoy fast driving.

( ) 3. Generally, I manage to keep a calm appearance even though I am upset inside.

( ) 4. There are too few people nowadays with enough courage to stand up for what is right.

( ) 5. Persons who tend to be 'bossy' actually lack self confidence although they may not realise it.

( ) 6. I do not like it when people are not clear about what I say and ask me to repeat it.

( ) 7. Effective leadership means to enable people to give the best to themselves rather than seek the best for themselves.

( ) 8. There is too much sex and violence on TV nowadays – it needs to be controlled.

( ) 9. Somewhere I have learned to have a positive, healthy attitude towards sex, my body, intimacy etc.

( ) 10. I find it difficult to stick to a diet; quit smoking etc.

( ) 11. In my opinion speed limits should be strongly enforced to avoid accidents.

( ) 12. Parents tend to be too permissive nowadays.

Fig. 4. Transactional analysis questionnaire (1).

( ) 13. I believe that absolute openness and honesty with others is possible.

( ) 14. In my opinion 95% of the important life decisions are based on feelings.

( ) 15. Too many persons these days allow others to push them around too much.

( ) 16. Although most people are not, I seem to be quite comfortable with a long period of silence.

( ) 17. I can recall situations where, as a child, older people made me feel ashamed.

( ) 18. There are times when one is justified in smacking a child for its own good.

( ) 19. We need more rather than less censorship of films, TV, magazines etc.

( ) 20. Even with strangers, I seldom feel bored, impatient or lonely.

( ) 21. I know that sometimes I ought to eat and drink less than I do.

( ) 22. The ceremony of baptism is much more than a symbolic ritual – it is essential for the spiritual welfare of the individual.

( ) 23. My parents encouraged me to explore and learn things for myself.

( ) 24. I find I become uncomfortable in 'unstructured' or 'unexpected' situations.

( ) 25. Even when one feels life is not worth living, no one is justified in committing suicide.

( ) 26. I attend more courses, seminars, lectures etc, than most people I know.

( ) 27. Sometimes I tell myself 'Shut up – you're talking too much.'

( ) 28. A remedy for the modern divorce situation would be to make the conditions for divorce more stringent so that marriage would be considered in a more serious light.

Fig. 4. Transactional analysis questionnaire (1) – continued.

( ) 29. I seldom, if ever, blush.

( ) 30. Most mistakes result from misunderstanding rather than carelessness.

( ) 31. When in a tense situation, I tend to laugh to relieve the situation.

( ) 32. Most youngsters, of both sexes, would benefit from obligatory military service.

( ) 33. I speak up for my strong convictions, but will change my mind in response to sound ideas.

( ) 34. Humility is one of the virtues, perhaps the greatest one.

( ) 35. Many men seem to compensate for small brains by having long hair.

( ) 36. Before starting some action I tend to gather facts and plan carefully beforehand, more so than others I know.

( ) 37. Marriages between people from different races or countries will invariably fail.

( ) 38. There are times when I allow myself to experience extreme periods of excitement and enjoyment.

( ) 39. Sometimes I hear myself say 'I do not make the rules, I just follow them.'

( ) 40. No matter how hard one tries, you cannot change human nature.

( ) 41. I do not believe that there has to be a natural and unresolvable conflict between organisations and individuals.

( ) 42. There are many times when I feel like skipping or running away.

( ) 43. The argument for capital punishment will never be completely done away with.

( ) 44. People nowadays should attend church more often.

( ) 45. More often than not I tend to estimate the risks of making a decision before making it.

Fig. 4. Transactional analysis questionnaire (1) – continued.

( ) 46. I tend to be concerned about approval of others, more so than I care to admit.

( ) 47. I like to run things; be 'boss of the situation', take charge.

( ) 48. Sometimes I have made myself unpopular in order to get an important job done.

( ) 49. I do not mind being a subordinate, but would like someone else as my superior.

( ) 50. I quickly become bored with a situation.

( ) 51. I believe that society would be better off if the laws were more rigorously enforced.

( ) 52. There are times when I cry unashamedly in the presence of others.

( ) 53. I tend to 'play down' others more than I should.

( ) 54. I tend to envy persons who quit their career in order to start a new life style.

( ) 55. I just cannot trust people like many seem to do.

( ) 56. I tend to prefer creative, as opposed to traditional solutions to the majority of problems.

( ) 57. If a situation appears to be overly serious, I am likely to attempt some humour to lessen the tension.

( ) 58. I am inclined to challenge others inquiringly and become aggressive.

( ) 59. It is my firm conviction that people are capable of sustained self-direction and control.

( ) 60. I cannot understand why some people take life so seriously – some playing once in while is good.

Fig. 4. Transactional analysis questionnaire (1) – continued.

USING TRANSACTIONAL ANALYSIS

The basic assumptions of transactional analysis are that:

- People learn at an early age ways of feeling and behaving that tend to become habitual regardless of their continued appropriateness.
- Feelings cause behaviour.
- Feelings and behaviour can be controlled. Where necessary the unproductive ones can be replaced with more acceptable ones.
- You can help other people to modify their feelings and behaviour.

In transactional analysis the individual's personality is seen as three **ego states**. An ego state is defined as a constant pattern of thinking and feeling attached to a pattern of behaving. With few exceptions, most of us have a dominant ego state which colours the way in which we communicate with others.

Understanding our ego states

Our self as parent

This means the part of the personality dealing mainly with values and opinions. There are two sub-groups:

(a) *Critical Parent* – only accepts a person if he/she agrees with their views or follows their instructions to the letter; tend to be critical of others and forceful in expressing their views. Verbal clues: 'should', 'ought', 'do', 'don't', 'never'.

(b) *Nurturing parent* – supportive of others; accepts others unconditionally. Verbal clues: 'Let me help you', 'Well done'.

Our self as adult

This means the rational part of the personality. It asks questions, gathers facts and makes decisions. Verbal clues: 'That's interesting.' 'Why?', 'How?' 'Who?'. 'Let's consider this.'

Our self as child

The emotional part of the personality. There are three sub-groups:

(a) Free or natural child – expresses feelings openly. Creative, spontaneous.

(b) Adapted child – rebellious or over submissive. The 'yes man' in all of us.

(c) Little professor – the know-all, precocious. Verbal clues: 'I want', 'I feel', 'I know'.

We all have something of each ego state in our personality, which will be expressed in different circumstances. When the appropriate ego state is used in response to what another person says, it is known as a **complementary transaction**, which means that both people are on the same wavelength, even though they may be in different ego states. The following are examples of such complementary transactions (figures 5 and 6):

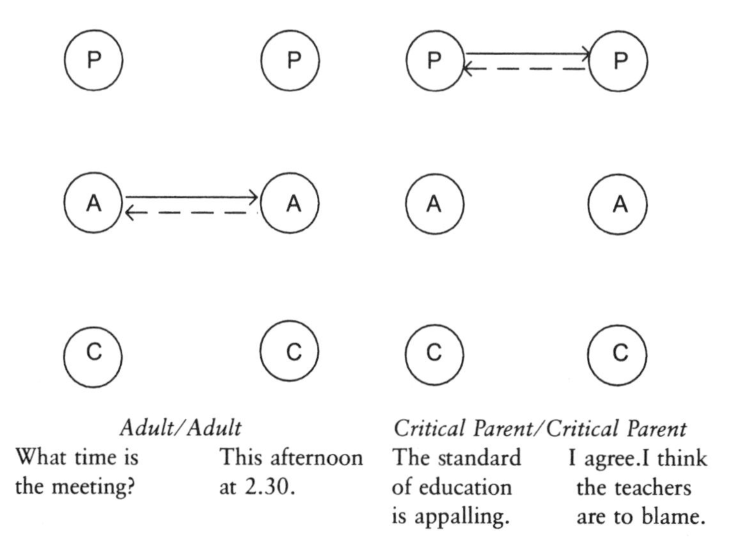

Fig. 5. Example of complementary transactions.

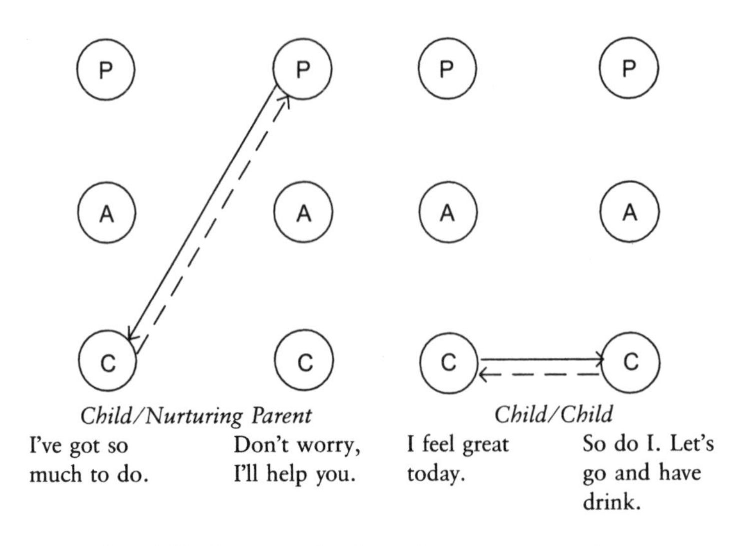

Fig. 6. Further example of complementary transactions.

However, when the response is inappropriate (not what the first speaker expected) it is called a **crossed transaction** as shown in the following examples:

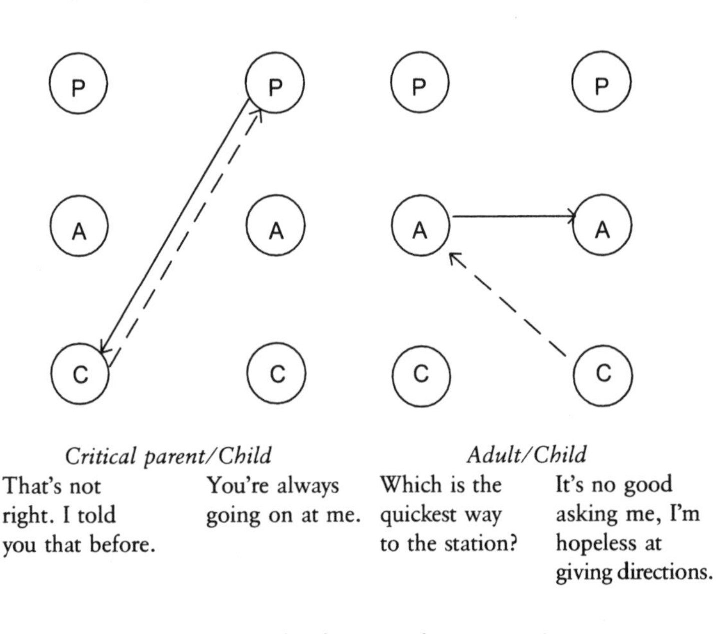

Fig. 7. Example of a 'crossed transaction'.

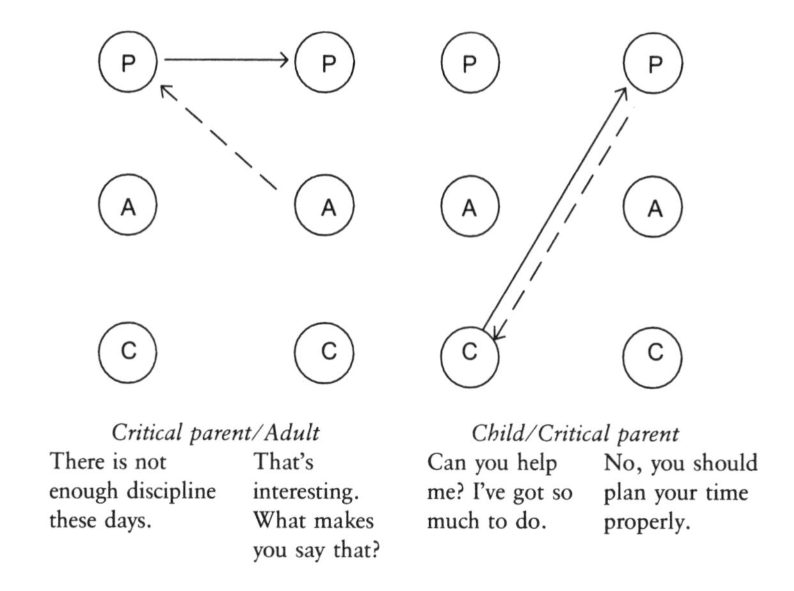

Fig. 8. Further example of 'crossed transaction'.

As Adult is the logical behaviour and is not subjected to emotion, it is the only ego state that can decide what is appropriate. Thus the Adult might decide that Adult, Parent or Child is the appropriate behaviour in any given situation.

Should you decide that the response you have received is inappropriate, then you can help the other person to change to a more acceptable ego state. This is called 'hooking'. You can hook people into another ego state simply by inviting them do so by what you say and how you say it.

Examples

To ADULT by:
- asking a question
- stating a fact
- asking for opinions.

To NURTURING PARENT by:
- asking for help
- asking for advice
- expressing your fears/concerns.

To CHILD by:
- being one yourself
- being enthusiastic
- going into Nurturing Parent
- being humorous about the situation.

As a counsellor, one should remain in the ADULT ego state, whilst at the same time allowing and acknowledging the emotions expressed by the client. The counsellor should then attempt to hook the client into an ADULT state, so that they can consider the problem and its implications logically.

Examples

Client:	'I'm really fed up with my boss. All he does is criticise and complain. Never a word of praise or thanks. He expects everyone to do exactly what he says without question as if we are a bunch of robots.'
Counsellor:	'You feel unhappy that your boss does not treat you as an individual or listen to your ideas?'
Client:	'Yes, I do.'
Counsellor:	'Why do you think he behaves like this?'

The counsellor allowed the client to express his views, listened, acknowledged the feelings and then attempted to hook the client into adult by asking a question.

Refer back to the questionnaire that you completed earlier. By following the scoring instructions as set out below, and constructing the graphs, you will reveal your preferred ego state, the one in which you feel most comfortable.

TRANSACTIONAL ANALYSIS
Profiles – Part 2

Instructions

Score one point for each statement you have answered with a +. Answers with a – do not score. On the next page plot the score totals P, A, C on the PAC diagram and by connecting the established points, you will have your PAC profile.

On the following page plot the numbers of your sub totals Pco, Pca, Pnu, Pov and Pcr on the Parent diagram and by connecting the points you will have the profile of your parent ego state. Likewise by plotting the sub totals Cna, Cad and Clp on the child diagram, you will produce the profile of your Child ego state.

	1 ( )		3 ( )	2 ( )
	4 ( )		7 ( )	6 ( )
	5 ( )		9 ( )	10 ( )
	8 ( )		13 ( )	14 ( )
Sub total Pco		( )	16 ( )	17 ( )
	11 ( )		20 ( )	21 ( )
	12 ( )		23 ( )	Sub total Cna ( )
	15 ( )		26 ( )	24 ( )
	18 ( )		29 ( )	27 ( )
Sub total Pca		( )	30 ( )	31 ( )
	19 ( )		33 ( )	34 ( )
	22 ( )		36 ( )	39 ( )
	25 ( )		38 ( )	42 ( )
	28 ( )		41 ( )	Sub total Cad ( )
			45 ( )	
Sub total Pnu		( )	52 ( )	46 ( )
	32 ( )		56 ( )	49 ( )
	35 ( )		48 ( )	54 ( )
	37 ( )		59 ( )	57 ( )
				60 ( )
	40 ( )		A =	Sub total Clp ( )
	43 ( )			C =
Sub total Ppa		( )		
	44 ( )			
	47 ( )			
	50 ( )			
	51 ( )			
Sub total Pov		( )		
	53 ( )			
	55 ( )			
	58 ( )			
Sub total Pcr		( )		
	P =			

Fig. 9. Transactional analysis questionnaire (2).

	Parent	Adult	Child	
100				100
	16	16		
			12	
90				90
	14			
80				80
		14	10	
70				70
	12			
60				60
		12		
			8	
50				50
	10			
40				40
30				30
	8	10		
			6	
20				20
	6			
		8		
			5	
10				10
	4	6	3	
0				0

Interpretation of scores

The ego state with the highest score indicates the one which is most favoured by you. If any of the scores are within two or three points of each other, you should find it quite easy to move between those ego states. There is no right or wrong 'best' ego state; try to use the most appropriate one for the situation.

PARENT DIAGRAM

concerned	caring	nurturing	prejudiced	over demanding	critical
4	4	4	5	4	4
3	3	3	4	3	3
2	2	2	2	2	2
1	1	1	1	1	1
0	0	0	0	0	0

CHILD DIAGRAM

natural	adapted	little professor
6	6	5
5	5	4
4	4	3
3	3	2
2	2	1
1	1	0
0	0	

Using a PAC Profile

The percentiles shown in the diagram mention your score as compared to the average score of a normal population. For instance, if you would score 13 on the parent scale this would mean that your score is higher than 80% of a normal population would score and is lower than 20% of a normal population would score.

Interpretation of your PAC profile

The highest percentile score of the 3 scores indicates that the ego state is most used by you. If there is a difference of 20 or more on the percentiles scale between the highest score and the second highest this means that the highest scoring ego state usage is dominant for you. If there is less than 20% difference then there is a likelihood that there is a switching back and forth between the two ego states of which phenomenon most persons are not consciously aware. It is suggested that you will get most insights by studying the composition of your parent and child profiles as there you may find data that will help you when consciously building up your adult ego state.

GIVING AND RECEIVING 'STROKES'

We acknowledge that all young children need stroking and similar forms of physical contact in order to survive. As people mature the need for such 'strokes' continues as a sign of recognition by others. Physical touching is less acceptable among adults in our society, so words and expression are used instead.

Strokes can be both positive and negative. Positive strokes such as 'Good morning', 'How are you today?', 'Thank you', or simply a smile, leave the recipient feeling good and positive about the giver. Negative strokes such as criticism or a frown makes the recipient feel unhappy and negative towards the speaker.

All strokes recognise the existence of an individual and it is better to receive negative strokes than no strokes at all.

Categories of strokes

Strokes of either category can be conditional or unconditional.

1. Positive unconditional – 'I like you'.'

2. Positive conditional – 'I like you if you do this for me.'

3. Negative conditional – 'I don't like you when you do that.'

4. Negative unconditional – 'I don't like you.'

Conditional strokes may be used to modify a person's behaviour. You may give an employee a positive conditional stroke for doing something well and a negative stroke when they are persistently late for work.

People receive strokes of all types, but are very apt to pass negative strokes on to others. For example, you may receive a negative stroke from your spouse before you leave for work in the morning. There is a good chance that you will give a negative stroke to the first person you contact at work.

Those people who regularly receive their quota of positive strokes are less likely to require counselling than those who regularly receive negative strokes or none at all. When conducting a counselling interview, it is quite in order to give positive strokes to the client, but never *negative* ones.

CASE STUDIES: EGO STATES OBSERVED

Identify each reaction by its correct ego state as either CP critical parent, NP nurturing parent, A adult, NC natural child or AC adapted child.

1. Late for work

One of your staff arrives late for the second time in a week and says:

(a) It's not my fault, I tried to get here on time but it did not work. ______

(b) It was such a nice morning I decided to walk. ______

(c) I'm sorry I'm late, I hope it has not caused too much of a problem. I'll soon catch up. ______

2. The cold office

You are sitting at your desk in your office when your secretary comes in and tells you that the heating has broken down. You say:

(a) We might as well go home. I'm not staying in a cold office. ______

(b) That's typical of the maintenance department. Get me the manager and I'll give him a piece of my mind. ______

(c) Please phone the maintenance department and tell them what has happened. ______

3. The complaint

A colleague complains to you that he has been passed over for a promotion for which he had applied. You say:

(a) Never mind, there will be other chances. Everything will work out in the end. ______

(b) That's nothing, you ought to hear how they treated me. ______

(c) Did you ask the reason why? ______

4. The disagreement

You have a disagreement with another manager which is overheard by a colleague who says:

(a) I hope you gave him what for. He deserves it. ______

(b) I really enjoyed listening to that. ______

(c) Do you feel OK after that? Let me get you a coffee. ______

Suggested responses are on page 96.

6
Counselling for Stress

WHAT IS STRESS?

We all live and work under pressures. Indeed, some element of pressure is necessary to motivate us in our thoughts and deeds. However, when the pressures become intolerable, chemical reactions take place within our bodies resulting in stress-related illnesses.

We all have different tolerance levels, so that events that cause stress in some people will be brushed aside by others. Some people are more prone to stress than others and this may be due to their personality or lifestyle. For example, people who tend to be competitive, aggressive, impatient, hasty or who feel powerless, rejected or threatened, are more likely to suffer stress than those who are calm, relaxed, considerate and sociable.

DETECTING THE SYMPTOMS OF STRESS

People under stress usually do their best to hide the fact from others, but the observant manager will detect signs that may indicate that a colleague or subordinate is feeling stressed.

Typical symptoms

Physical symptoms
Nervous twitching.
Dry mouth and throat.
Headaches.
Indigestion.
Sweating.
Tiredness.
Breathing irregularities.
Tense muscles.
Fidgeting.
Diarrhoea/constipation.

Behavioural symptoms
Feeling
- restless
- easily irritated
- quick tempered
- misunderstood
- a failure
- unable to cope
- upset, worried, tearful
- demotivated

Difficulty in
- concentrating
- making decisions
- thinking clearly

Loss of
- memory
- creativity
- interest in self and others
- vitality and energy

Workplace symptoms
Reduced performance
Communication breakdown
Lower job satisfaction
Poor decision making
Focus on unproductive tasks

Stress related illnesses are one of the major causes of absenteeism and cost British industry many millions of pounds each year.

UNDERSTANDING THE CAUSES OF STRESS

Every year we seem to experience more and more pressure, much of it exerted by people and events beyond our control. As a result an increasing number of people suffer from stress and its associated physical and mental illnesses. Until quite recently, stress was considered to be a 'character weakness' and thus people were reluctant to talk about their problems. Now it is accepted to be a

HOLMES AND RAHE – SOCIAL ADJUSTMENT SCALE

	Event	*Rating Points*
1	Death of a spouse	100
2	Divorce	73
3	Marital separation	65
4	Prison term	63
5	Death of a close family member	63
6	Personal injury or illness	53
7	Marriage	50
8	Loss of job	47
9	Marital reconciliation	45
10	Retirement	45
11	Change of health of family member	44
12	Pregnancy	40
13	Sex difficulties	39
14	Gain of new family member	39
15	Business readjustment	39
16	Change in financial state	38
17	Death of close friend	37
18	Change to different type of work	36
19	Increased arguments with spouse	35
20	Large mortgage or loan	30
21	Foreclosure of mortgage or loan	30
22	Change in responsibilities at work	29
23	Son or daughter leaving home	29
24	Trouble with in-laws	29
25	Outstanding personal achievement	28

Fig. 10. The Social Adjustment Scale (Holmes & Rahe).

genuine cause of many illnesses. Most forward-thinking companies and organisations are making attempts to reduce the **stressors** (stress factors) within their workplace. Some even offer professional counselling for employees who feel stressed.

Most of the causes of stress are domestic in origin; they are then exacerbated by pressures at work. These extra pressures are in turn taken home where they are added to the existing problems. This results in a vicious circle of ever increasing stress which – if not diagnosed and treated – can in extreme cases lead to mental breakdown and even suicide.

The Social Adjustment Scale (Holmes and Rahe)

In the 1960s, two American psychologists, Holmes and Rahe, studied the causes of stress and as a result prepared their Social Adjustment Scale which listed the prime causes of potential stress that a person may experience from changes to their life. In order to make comparisons of importance, each event was given rating points. The top 25 events are shown in figure 10.

With economic changes that have taken place in recent years, events relating to redundancy and financial problems are likely to feature nearer the top of any similar scale produced today. Increasing crime and vandalism also cause great stress to victims and potential victims.

Everyone in modern organisations is under increasing pressure, from the Chief Executive down. How stressful is your work environment? Recently a questionnaire was published in the *New York Times* designed to help people determine the stress level of their own working environments. This questionnaire is reproduced in figure 11. Read each statement and tick if it is applicable to your workplace. Once you have completed this, calculate the score according to the Scoring Sheet.

QUESTIONNAIRE

Determining the stress levels in your own workplace

Group A

____ Company has been taken over recently
____ Staff reductions/lay offs in past year
____ Recent department/company reorganisations
____ Staff expect company to be sold or relocated
____ Employee benefits significantly cut recently
____ Mandatory overtime frequently required
____ Employees have little control over how they work
____ Consequences of making mistakes are severe
____ Workloads vary greatly
____ Most work is machine-paced or fast-paced
____ Staff must react quickly and accurately to change
____ Personal conflicts are commonplace

Group B

____ Few available opportunities for advancement
____ Red tape hinders things getting done
____ Inadequate staffing, money or technology
____ Pay is below the going rate
____ Sick and vacation benefits are below the norm
____ Employees are rotated between shifts
____ New machines/work methods have been introduced recently
____ Noise/vibration levels are high or temperature keeps changing
____ Employees normally isolated from one another
____ Performance or work units normally below average

Group C

____ Employees have little or no privacy
____ Meal breaks are unpredictable
____ Work is either sedentary or physically exhausting
____ If on flexitime, you regularly change start and finish times

Fig. 11. Determining the stress levels in your own organisation.

Group D

____ Staff recognised and rewarded for their contributions
____ Management takes firm action to reduce stress
____ Mental health benefits are provided
____ Company has formal employee communication programme
____ Staff given information on coping with stress
____ Staff given clear job descriptions
____ Management and staff talk openly with one another
____ Employees are free to talk to each other

Group E

____ Work rules are published and are the same for everybody
____ Child care programmes are available
____ Employees can work flexible hours
____ Perks are granted freely
____ Employees have access to necessary technology
____ Staff and management trained in resolving conflicts
____ Staff receive training when assigned new tasks
____ Company encourages work and personal support groups
____ Staff have place and time for relaxation

Group F

____ Staff assistance programme is available
____ Each employee's work space is not crowded
____ Staff can put up personal items in their workplace
____ Management appreciate humour in the workplace
____ Retirement programmes are available

Fig. 11. Determining the stress levels in your own organisation – continued.

Scoring Sheet

For each statement ticked, assign the following scores:

Group A – 3 points
Group B – 2 points
Group C – 1 point

Total these scores. The higher the score, the greater the cause of stress exists.

Group D – 3 points
Group E – 2 points
Group F – 1 point

Total these scores. The higher the score, the more the company tries to reduce stress.

Subtract the second total from the first. The result may vary from minus 50 points for extremely good working conditions to plus 60 for a very high stress environment.

+60 Dangerously high stress environment

+50

+40 Stress level needs to be addressed quickly

+30

+20 Stress level acceptable to most people

+10

0 Some pressure but little stress

–10

–20 Company recognises that stress reduces ability

–30

–40

–50 Excellent, stress-free working conditions

Fig. 11. Determining the stress levels in your own organisation – continued.

Different occupations have built-in levels of stress, of which people should be aware before they pursue certain careers. Professor Cary Cooper and six colleagues evaluated jobs on a ten point scale. Below is a sample of their findings, starting with the most stressful occupations and ending with the least.

Stress levels by occupation

8.3	miner	6.2	teacher
7.7	police	5.8	commercial manager
7.5	civil airline pilot		professional sports person
	prison officer	5.5	selling
	construction worker	4.8	farming
	journalist	4.7	armed forces
7.2	actor	4.3	accountant
6.8	doctor		engineer
6.5	nurse/midwife		secretary/receptionist
6.3	fireman	3.7	computing
	musician	2.0	librarian

Fig. 12. Stress levels by occupation.

COUNSELLING FOR STRESS AT WORK

As an observant manager, you may identify symptoms of stress in a member of your staff and decide to initiate a counselling interview. On no account should you ever suggest or imply to that person that they are suffering from stress, for the chances are that they will immediately deny it and become defensive.

Your task is to discover the reason for the stress and help the person to reach an acceptable and workable solution.

A 7-point plan

1. Use the techniques previously described to reach the core problem.
2. Encourage the client to explore their feelings about the problem.
3. Keep the problem client-orientated.
4. Help the client to suggest solutions and to discuss the consequences of each one.
5. Do not pursue external problems unless you have special qualifications to do so.
6. Offer information where appropriate.
7. If the only solution appears to be a change in company procedure or policy, admit that this is beyond the control of both you and your client. In such a case look for secondary solutions which may ease the situation.

POINTS FOR DISCUSSION

1. What do you consider to be the main stress factor in your own workplace? How do these factors show themselves in the behaviour of other employees?

2. How do you rate your own levels of stress? Do you think understanding the causes could help you reduce the levels?

3. From your own experience, give three examples of how stress has

   (a) caused problems in the organisation

   (b) generated positive or creative outcomes.

7
Types of Counselling

Whatever the reason for a counselling interview, the techniques are common to all. However, the objective of each specific interview will determine the approach taken by the counsellor. The purpose of this chapter is to provide a guide to the appropriate direction to take and questions to ask in a variety of situations.

COUNSELLING AT APPRAISALS

The annual, formal appraisal interview provides the manager with the ideal opportunity to practise counselling skills. Whilst there are numerous appraisal systems (see *How to Conduct Staff Appraisals* in this series) the objective in each case is

- to review the employee's performance since the last appraisal,
- to agree tasks and standards for the future.

Counselling can play an important role when the appraisee has failed to reach pre-agreed targets, goals or standards. In such cases the object is *not* to criticise or punish the person (negative) but to discover the reasons why the person has not been successful, and so help them to improve (positive).

When moving into 'counselling mode', you must remember to be both neutral and objective. You can achieve this by adopting an open relaxed posture, and by asking questions in an unemotional tone of voice. Be careful not to introduce words such as 'difficulties', 'problems' or 'failure' as the employee may take these as criticisms.

Example

An ideal open question might: 'At the last appraisal we agreed that you would increase your sales turnover by 10%. How did you set about achieving this?' There is no hint of criticism or failure, simply a question. The answer to it should provide the manager with valuable information about the employee's attitude and behaviour to the target.

A note of caution: this approach should not be taken if the targets or goals are assigned to the employee without prior consultation, since the answer will be along the lines of, 'I told you that 10% was impossible at the time.'

Helping the individual

When seeking solutions to improve future performance, under no circumstances compare the employee's efforts with those of higher achieving colleagues as this could undermine the employee's confidence. If a solution is to have any chance of success, it must come from the employee. Having explored the pros and cons, the employee must be allowed to act upon the solution even though it may not be one that the manager agrees with or even approves.

Remember, nobody fails 'just for the hell of it.' There is always a reason, which by applying sound counselling techniques will be revealed. Reasons may include any of the following:

- Changes in the market – shrinking; taste; technology.
- Lack of motivation – ineffective management; insufficient training; poor career development.
- Personality – relationship with colleagues.
- External – domestic; financial; health.

Counselling is not about directing, persuading or manipulating. Do not pretend to be 'counselling' if you are planning to steer the person toward a solution that you really wish to impose.

CAREER COUNSELLING

Some recent research

During the summer of 1993, research was undertaken on career guidance. Among the findings were:

(a) Assessments help people to understand where they are and the direction they could take.

(b) Such assessments should be done by assessors who are

independent from the person's current employer. The reason is that anyone trying to assess or guide an employee or subordinate will find it difficult to remain objective, while they have the needs of the company foremost in their mind.

(c) People should enjoy both their work and their private lives.

(d) Some industries suffer from 'image problems'. This has little or nothing to do with the product but the way in which it is promoted.

(e) Fewer people today consider long term careers. This is particularly true for those under forty years of age.

(f) It is difficult to keep people motivated long term.

'We hire people for their technical skills. We fire people for their behaviour faults.' This quote from an advertisement for a seminar on psychometric testing just about sums up the attitude of most employers today.

Whilst having regard to (b) above, many managers are expected to take on the role of career counsellors for their staff. In many instances this is incorporated into the appraisal interview.

Using a questionnaire

Before embarking upon a career counselling interview, it is a good idea to ask the counsellee to complete a simple questionnaire. This will provide the manager with information about the employee's thinking as far as his/her career is concerned.

The manager/counsellor can use the answers given to the questionnaire to formulate the right approach. Elaboration and specific questions are always good openers (see page 82):

Examples

'I see that what you least like about your present job is the lack of opportunities to use your initiative. What do you feel restricts this?'

'You mentioned that you are motivated by responsibility and this need is not being satisfied. How do you think *we* can improve this?'

Counselling may well indicate that it is in the best interests of the client to pursue a career outside the company. If this is the case, then as the manager you ought not to hinder this even though the person is a valuable employee.

Below is an example of the type of questions which can be included:

CAREER QUESTIONNAIRE

1. What do you like most about your current job?__________
2. What do you like least about your current job?__________
3. What would you like to do that you don't already do?____
4. Why did you choose your present job?__________
5. Where do you see yourself in 3 years' time?__________
6. What are you currently doing to achieve this?__________
7. What are your hobbies and interests?__________
8. Which, if any, would you like to pursue as a career?____
9. How could you achieve this?__________
10. Which of the following motivates you the most? Money/ Recognition/Security/Responsibility/Promotional Prospects/ Good Work Relationship:__________
11. How well is this motivator being addressed at present?
Non-existent 1 2 3 4 5 6 Completely
12. Briefly describe your ideal career path.__________

Note: In addition to the above, if the counselling is being carried out by an independent counsellor, there would be questions about qualifications, skills and career progression to date.

Fig. 13. Example of a career questionnaire.

Points to remember

- Avoid giving the employee false hopes and promises.
- If you truly believe that the employee's aspirations are well beyond his abilities, make sure that he or she is fully aware of everything that must be done to achieve his ambition.
- Provide help in the form of information, details of training courses, books to read, people and organisations that may help.
- If you help and encourage the person, they will think well of you. If you hinder them, they will resent you.

Using psychometric assessments

Psychometric assessments should only be carried out by qualified, licensed assessors. A wide selection of such assessments is commercially available, some better than others. Many of them purport to provide the assessee with a character profile under such headings as stability, dependability, ambition, motivation, sociability and so on. Others consider such traits as aggression, logical thinking and supportiveness of others.

Such assessments can provide useful data about a person. However, it can be dangerous to base a future career only upon such information.

REDUNDANCY COUNSELLING

This can be an extremely difficult task for managers, since it is hard to remain objective in such circumstances. Both people will know each other, extremely conscious of the fact that one still has a job while the other does not.

It is very rare for someone who has been made redundant not to feel resentment against the company. It is usually easier for the person to express their anger against an individual than an inanimate body and in such a case this is likely to be you.

As this anger will surface at some point during the interview, why not invite the person to vent their spleen right at the start. Open with a question such as 'How did you feel when you were told that you were being made redundant?' This may well prompt a highly emotional outburst but at least you will be ready for it. Listen carefully and don't say anything until the person has really finished.

Then simply reflect back the main feeling expressed. 'You feel extremely angry.'

Until the individual has had the chance to get their feelings off their chest, it will not be possible to proceed in a constructive way. If the client is of an age, say under 45, with a good prospect of continuing their career elsewhere, the counselling can take the form of career guidance. However, with older people it may be necessary to investigate other avenues. These can include:

- Their financial status and commitments.
- Other sources of income, investment, spouse's income.
- Self-employment, consultancy.
- Early retirement, part-time work.
- Professional counselling.

It is extremely regrettable that during the past few years, so many companies seeking to reduce costs turned to redundancy as the easy option. Many companies, having shed themselves of vast pools of experience, are now realising the error of their ways.

Practical guidelines

When faced with conducting a redundancy counselling interview, points to remember are:

- Be empathetic *not* sympathetic.
- Be honest and open.
- Remain neutral and unemotional.

One of the most unpleasant experiences faced a certain manager recently. He was directed to undertake redundancy interviews with five members of his team, knowing that he himself would be made redundant six months later.

CORRECTION COUNSELLING

I have purposely used the word correction instead of discipline as the objective should be to correct (put right) the problem, to ensure that it does not recur – not to punish the person for having transgressed.

In these instances, it will be the manager who calls for the interview and it is very important to obtain as much information as possible about the incident before starting the interview.

In order to achieve this, it will be vital to get to the core problem by using the techniques previously suggested. As manager you may well have a bank of solutions, but in order to have a chance of it working long term, the solution must come from the client.

Monitoring progress

Once a solution has been agreed upon, you will need to set up a system for monitoring progress. The usual method is to arrange a number of informal meetings, weekly, monthly or whatever timescale is appropriate, to review the situation. It is during these meetings that the manager can offer additional help (not advice) as necessary.

GRIEVANCE COUNSELLING

This is conducted along similar lines to correction counselling; the objective is to ensure that the core problem is resolved.

Where the grievance is the result of conflict between two or more colleagues, each party should be counselled separately and then brought together for a conciliatory meeting.

Should the grievance be between one of your employees and a more senior member of the company, or someone over whom you have no authority, counsel your staff member and get their agreement for you to explain to the other person, and their manager if appropriate, exactly what you have done and why.

PERSONAL PROBLEM COUNSELLING

As previously suggested, it is very unlikely that you will feel either qualified or inclined to pursue such matters. All you can do is to provide information about people and organisations who may be able to help.

Depending on the circumstances these might include for example:

- Money problems – Money Advice Centres, Citizens Advice Bureau, local bank/building society manager, accountant/book-keeper.

- Marital problems – Relate, local GP.
- Legal problems – Citizens Advice Bureau, local Law Centres, the Legal Aid Board, the Law Society, solicitor.
- Medical problems – local health centre.
- Housing – Department of Social Security, Citizens Advice Bureau.
- Alcohol abuse – local health centre, Alcoholics Anonymous, Al-Anon.

CASE STUDIES

The following case studies illustrate some of the benefits of good counselling at work.

Ralph and the new machine

Ralph joined his company as a maintenance engineer. Having previous experience of the existing machines, he quickly proved to be a very competent engineer.

Some six months later, a brand new piece of equipment was installed by the company. Pressures of work meant that Ralph and his colleagues only received a brief practical training on the new machine. Each engineer was given a comprehensive technical manual to study to help them to familiarise themselves with the new machine. A couple months passed before Ralph's manager, Bob, noticed that Ralph avoided working on the new equipment, preferring to keep to the older machines.

This concerned Bob, and he decided to try and find out the reason for this. He arranged a meeting and began by praising Ralph for his efficiency, before broaching the subject of the new machines. At first Ralph was reluctant to talk about it. However, Bob used his counselling skills and eventually uncovered the core problem. Ralph suffered from dyslexia and found it very hard to read the manual and was too embarrassed to tell anyone.

Bob asked if more practical training would help, to which Ralph readily agreed. He also informed Ralph that evening classes were available to help people with dyslexia. Ralph was very relieved to have had the opportunity to discuss his disability in private and that the criticism and ridicule that he had feared, had not happened.

Sally's career in sales

Sally worked as a telesalesperson in a frozen food company. For the first year she worked well and was among the top telesalespeople. Then her supervisor noticed that Sally's enthusiasm was waning and that she was not performing as well.

The supervisor discussed her concern about Sally's performance with her manager. The manager decided to counsel Sally about her career. At the interview Sally revealed that she was becoming bored with her job. Further questioning showed that she enjoyed selling but would much prefer to be 'on the road'.

The manager agreed to discuss this with one of the Field Sales Managers and three months later Sally attended an internal sales training course to prepare her for her new career.

If the company had operated an appraisal system, this problem could have been picked up and acted upon at an earlier stage, to the benefit of both Sally and the company.

Nick – the late progress chaser

Nick was employed as a progress chaser with his company. He was a diligent although not exceptional employee, and was noted for his good time-keeping.

Suddenly Nick began to arrive at work anything up to an hour late. His manager let this go for two or three weeks to see if it was only a temporary blip. However, when the lateness persisted, the manager decided to talk to Nick about it.

During the first part of the interview Nick gave a string of excuses such as car trouble, bad weather, feeling tired and so on. The manager knew that these were only 'presenting problems' and continued to question Nick.

Eventually Nick confessed that the real reason was that his wife had left him and he was having to take the children to a child minder. Although this was an area beyond the experience of the manager, he empathised with Nick's problem and asked him to think about possible solutions. Nick suggested that he leave the company and take part-time work, but agreed that this was not a practical solution. It transpired that Nick had not even told his parents about his problem. After much heart searching he came to the conclusion that he should discuss the matter with his mother and father and ask for their help.

It was agreed that Nick would meet with his manager in a month's time to review the situation and in the meantime he would do his best to get to work as soon as possible each day and work part of his lunchtime. At Nick's request, the manager agreed not to mention the problem to anyone else.

Moira feels rejected

Moira was the secretary to the Production Director in a light engineering company. She had joined the company several years previously as a clerk/typist. Her first promotion came two years later when she became the new secretary to one of the Regional Sales Managers.

When the present position became vacant eighteen months ago, Moira applied and after two stringent interviews, was offered the job. Although her relationship with her boss was very formal, she enjoyed the work as she was given considerable freedom to make decisions and use her initiative.

Lately, however, Moira began to feel rather depressed and hard done by. She knew that it was no good trying to talk to the Production Director as his people management skills were virtually nil.

One day the Personnel Director approached Moira and asked her to come to his office to discuss a few points about the production workers' bonuses. After the business of the meeting had been concluded, Moira was about to leave when the Personnel Director said that he had noticed that she had not been her buoyant self lately and was there anything she would like to talk about. At first Moira was nonplussed, but then, realising that such an opportunity might not occur again, accepted his invitation.

After some general chat about her job and the company, Moira revealed the real reason for feeling the way that she did. The reason may appear trivial to many people but to Moira it was important. Recently the other directors had promoted their secretaries to Personal Assistant. It was only a change in title but for some reason, the Production Director had failed to follow suit. Moira agreed that this made her feel rejected and inferior. This was a problem to which Moira could offer no solution as it was out of her hands. Surprisingly enough, three days later Moira's director invited her to lunch, apologised for the oversight, retitled her position and posted a notice that effect on the company notice board.

This was a case where someone gave the impression of being unapproachable but was quite human after all.

Don

Don worked for a large retail chain and was the manager of a branch in a small country town. He had been with the company since he left school; he was now 31 and had held his present position for five years. Although he was reasonably content with life, and ran a profitable store, Don felt rather hard done by as he constantly seemed to be passed by when it came to promotion to a larger branch.

One day Don received an unexpected visit from his Regional Manager, Mike. Over lunch in a local pub, the manager asked Don if everything was alright.

'Yes of course it is. Why?' Don replied defensively.

'It's just that I noticed that you are on your third pint, and before you rarely had more than a half,' Mike said quietly.

'I just fancied it,' came the truculent response.

Mike immediately recognised the danger signals. He thought that a counselling session was in order to discover the reasons for Don's change of behaviour. Changing the subject, Mike asked after Don's family.

'They're OK I suppose,' Don said morosely.

'How are the children doing at school?' Mike asked. Don's tone had suggested that all was not OK.

'Oh they're both getting along quite well in the circumstances,' Don replied.

'And how's Linda?' Mike continued, referring to Don's wife. A few moments passed before Don spoke.

'Alright. She's pregnant again,' he said.

'You must feel pleased about that,' Mike said brightly.

'I would be if Linda didn't keep going on about money,' Don was beginning to open up.

'Money?' Mike reflected.

'Yes, she keeps on about me not getting promotion and feels that we're stuck in this place for the rest of our lives.' Was this the real reason for Don's behaviour? Although the pub was not the right place to undertake counselling, Mike decided to pursue the point.

'You feel disappointed that you have not been promoted recently,' he said.

'Yes, I do. I keep applying but am always rejected,' Don said aggressively.

'Why do you think that is?' Mike asked.

'I don't know,' came the reply.

'What could you do to improve your chances?'

'I really don't know. I try my best.'

'When did you last attend a management course?' Mike questioned.

'About four years ago, I think.'

'Do you think more training would help?'

'It can't do any harm, I suppose.' Don sounded more positive.

'I'll send you details of the next appropriate courses. Let me know if you would like to attend any of them. Also, before you apply for another promotion, I'm always available if you would like a chat. I have always considered you to be a good asset to the company and would certainly like to see you progress.' Mike realised that this was not an ideal conclusion but at least Don was in a more positive frame of mind and knew that help was available.

8
Counselling Checklists

1. ROLE OF THE MANAGER IN COUNSELLING

- Recognising and understanding – recognising the signs indicating problems.
- Empowering – enabling the employee to recognise the problem and encouraging them to talk about it.
- Resourcing – managing the problem which will include deciding who is best qualified to act as counsellor and to provide information.

2. WHERE COUNSELLING CAN BE APPLIED IN THE WORK-PLACE

- Managing effectiveness – appropriate counselling can prevent under performance; improve morale and motivation; reduce absenteeism.
- Increasing commitment – effective counselling can demonstrate the organisation's commitment to create loyalty and enthusiasm among the workforce.
- Improving self-development – workplace counselling can be used to give employees the confidence and encouragement to take responsibility for their self-development and career progression.
- Problem identification – recognising that a problem exists is an essential part of workplace counselling, both observing behaviour and listening to intuition.

3. BASIC SKILLS FOR COUNSELLING

- The ability to listen actively and obtain the real causes by questioning, evaluating, interpreting and supporting.
- Being sensitive to individual beliefs and values, some of which may be based on a different culture or religion.
- Having the ability to understand the problem from the client's point of view.
- Ability to empathise with the client's feelings and anxieties.
- To remain impartial, non-judgmental, and to refrain from giving advice.
- Having a genuine interest in the client's problem and showing one's sincerity.
- Treat the client as a unique individual who has the ability to solve their problem, if necessary with help.

4. PREPARING FOR THE INTERVIEW

- Select a place to talk that is quiet, free from interruption and not open to view.
- Research as much as possible before the interview.
- Allow sufficient time for the interview. If there is a time limit, tell the counsellee at the outset.
- Consider how you are going to introduce your perception of the situation.
- Be prepared for the client to have different expectations of the session; they may expect you to provide solutions.
- Remember that the client's view of the facts will be more important than the facts themselves and their behaviour may hide their true feelings.

5. CONDUCTING THE INTERVIEW

- Assure the person that matters of confidentiality will be treated as such.
- Give appropriate reassurances where necessary.
- Encourage the client to consider statements more deeply.
- Ask the client to clarify statements you do not understand.
- Take the initiative in probing areas which may be embarrassing and which you would both prefer to avoid.
- Remember that some points may be very important to the client that they will have to be discussed several times.
- If the client appears to become defensive, try to discover the reason and relax the pressure by changing your approach.
- Summarise the conversation and reflect back in your own words your understanding of what is being said.
- Identify emotions and reflect back what you believe to be the client's feelings.
- At the close of the session, clarify any decisions reached and agree what follow-up support will be useful.
- Recognise when a problem is one that cannot be resolved without expert, specialised help and offer appropriate information to the client.

6. DANGERS TO AVOID

- Realise that you may not like the client and be on guard against the possible problems this may cause.
- Avoid taking sides or becoming emotional.
- Repeating problems does not solve them.
- Resist the temptation to talk about your own problems, even if they appear similar to those of the client.
- Do not give advice, only information.
- Avoid directing the client towards solutions that will satisfy you.

Appendix

Suggested Answers to Case Studies

CHAPTER 2

Both (c) and (d) could be appropriate responses. In the latter case, a simple reflection such as, 'You feel angry about that question' may well result in the person telling you why they are angry.

CHAPTER 3

Page 22

1. How did you feel after the interview?

2. What do you most like about your job?

3. How are you getting on with your work colleagues?

4. What do you do to relax after work?

5. What part of your job do you find the most difficult? . . . Why is that?

Page 25

(a) You believe that you are not progressing as quickly as you would wish.

(b) You feel that your talents are not being fully utilised.

(c) You think that your ideas are not taken seriously.

(d) What makes you feel that?

(e) You feel that the company does not have a defined career structure.

(f) You believe that the company does not show sufficient concern for its staff.

Note
(d) is a difficult statement to reflect without appearing critical and a simple question to gain specific facts would be more appropriate.

Page 43
Always get as many facts about a situation as possible and then, if you believe it to be appropriate, move to option (b).

CHAPTER 4

Whilst (b) or (d) may relieve the situation momentarily, nothing has been done to reduce the apparent feelings of that person. The best option is (f) using a phrase such as 'You feel concerned about this meeting.'

CHAPTER 5

1. (a) AC (b) NC (c) NP

2. (a) NC (b) CP (c) A

3. (a) NP (b) AC (c) A

4. (a) AC (b) NC (c) NP

Glossary

Active listening. Indicating to the speaker by sounds and gestures that one is listening.

Appraisal interview. A formal meeting between a manager and one of his/her staff to review performance and set goals. Often provides an ideal opportunity for counselling.

Attitude. The behaviours of a person towards another person, persons or task.

Aural communication. Another term for **active listening.**

Behaviour. The way a person acts as a result of their feelings.

Body language. Non verbal communication expressed in the form of gestures and postures.

Client. Another term for counsellee.

Closed questions. Ones that only require a yes or no answer; usually begin with a verb, *eg* Can? Do? May?

Continuation behaviour. Sounds and signals encouraging the speaker to continue.

Core problem. The real underlying reason for changes in behaviour or attitude.

Counselling. Listening to another person's problems, empathising and helping that person to solve their problem.

Counsellee. Person being counselled.

Counsellor. Person conducting a counselling interview.

Ego state. The personality types identified by transactional analysis: Parent, Adult and Child.

Empathy. Acknowledgement of a person's feelings without associating oneself with the feelings or the problem.

Eye contact. Looking directly at the other person during conversations; it indicates interest in the person and what they are saying.

Leading question. One that guides the listener to the expected answer, *eg* 'You would agree, wouldn't you?'

Open question. One that invites an informative answer; begins with words such as Which? What? Where? How?

Oral communication. A term for speaking as opposed to written communication.

Personality. The way a person behaves under 'normal' circumstances, often categorised as 'introvert', 'extrovert', 'aggressive', 'submissive', and so on.

Presenting problem. The apparent or surface cause for a change in a person's behaviour or attitude.

Psychometric tests. Written questions designed to test a person's numeracy, skills and spatial awareness; also used to identify a person's personality profile and suitability for a specific job or post.

Reflection. Response by a counsellor, summarising the facts and/or feelings to a statement made by a client.

Stress. The point at which pressure becomes intolerable.

Sympathy. Identifying with another person's feeling, *eg* 'I know how you feel.'

Tone. Verbal emphasis which can indicate meaning.

Transactional analysis. A method of analysing verbal communication, designed to show how to reduce conflict.

Useful Contacts

NATIONAL ORGANISATIONS

Al-Anon, 1 Great Dover Street, London SE1 4YF. Tel: (0171) 483 0888.

Alcoholics Anonymous, PO Box 1, Stonebow House, YO1 2NT. Tel: York 644026

British Association for Counselling, 1 Regent Place, Rugby, Warks CV21 2PJ. Tel: (01788) 550899.

British Association for Commercial & Industrial Education (BACIE), 35 Harbour Exchange Square, London E14 9GE. Tel: (0171) 987 8989.

British Institute of Management, Cottingham Road, Corby. Tel: Corby 204222.

Citizens Advice Bureaux (National Association Headquarters), 115 Pentonville Road, London N1 9LP. Tel: (0171) 833 2181. Branches in most major towns and cities.

Department of Social Security (DSS), Headquarters Offices, London SW1A 2LN. Tel: (0171) 210 5983. Or see local telephone directories.

Employment Service (Headquarters), St Vincent House, Orange Street, London WC2 7HH. Tel: (0171) 273 3000. Or see local telephone directories.

Law Centres Federation, Duchess House, Warren Street, London W1P 5DA. Tel: (0171) 387 8570.

Institute of Family Therapy, 43 New Cavendish Street, London W1M 7RN. Tel: (0171) 935 1651.

Institute of Personnel & Development, Camp House, Wimbledon, London SW19 4UX. Tel: (0181) 946 9100. The professional body for human resource managers. Publishes a wide range of practical handbooks.

Law Society, 113 Chancery Lane, London WC2A 1PL. Tel: (0171) 242 1222. The solicitors' governing body.

National Association of Bereavement Services, 20 Norton Folgate, London E1 6DB. Tel: (0171) 247 0617.

National Association of Family Mediation & Conciliation Services, 156 Blackfriars Road, London SE1 8EN. Tel: (0171) 721 7647.

Relate Marriage Guidance, National Headquarters, Herbert Gray College, Little Church Street, Rugby CV21 3AP. Tel: Rugby 573241.

Samaritans (Central London Headquarters), 46 Marshall Street, London W1V 1LR. Tel: (0171) 734 2800. Or see local telephone directories.

LOCAL INFORMATION

Two of the best sources of local information are:

1. Citizens Advice Bureau.

2. Local public reference library.

Both will be able to assist with obtaining the names, addresses and telephone numbers of local help organisations of every kind.

Further Reading

Codependency in the Workplace: A Guide for Employee Assistance and Human Resource Professionals, Seth Allcorn (Quorum Books, London, 1992).

Counselling: A Practical Guide for Employers, Michael Megranahan (Institute of Personnel & Development, 1989).

Counselling for Managers: An Introductory Guide, John-Michael Hughes (BACIE, 1991).

Counselling People at Work, Robert De Board (Gower Press/ Wildwood House, 1987).

Counselling the Poor Performer, Hugh Fitzwilliams (Gower, 1991).

How to Conduct Staff Appraisals, Nigel Hunt (How To Books, 2nd edition 1994).

How to Manage People at Work, John Humphries (2nd edition 1995).

The Manager's Guide to Counselling at Work, Michael Reddy (British Psychological Society/Methuen, 1987).

Managing Difficult Staff, Helga Drummond (Kogan Page, 1990).

Personal Problems at Work: Counselling as a Resource for the Manager (British Association for Counselling).

Psychological Testing: A Practical Guide to Aptitude and Other Tests, J Toplis, V Dulewicz & C Fletcher (Institute of Personnel & Development, 1987).

Redundancy Counselling for Managers, Giles Burrows (Institute of Personnel & Development, 1985).

Index

How to Manage People at Work
John Humphries

'These days, if a textbook on people management is to succeed, it must be highly informative, reliable, comprehensive – and eminently user-friendly. Without doubt, *How to Manage People at Work* is one such book. Written in an attractive style that should appeal to any first-line manager who has neither the time nor the energy to cope with heavy reading, John Humphries has tackled his extremely wide subject ably and well. Rightly or wrongly, it has always been my experience that one has only to read the first couple of pages of any textbook on people management to discover whether or not the author enjoys an empathy with the people at the sharp end – and here is one author who, for my money, has passed the test with flying colours.' *Progress/NEBS Management Association.*

160pp illus. 1 85703 068 0. 2nd edition.

How to Conduct Staff Appraisals
Nigel Hunt

Managers and organisations neglect staff appraisal at their peril today. But what exactly is staff appraisal? Is it something to be welcomed or feared? Why is it now so vital, and what are the benefits? Should senior as well as junior staff undergo appraisal, and how could this be done? Which managers should do the appraisals, and how should they start? This book, now in a new edition, sets out a basic framework which every manager can use or adapt, whether in business and industry, transport, education, health and public services. Nigel Hunt is a consultant in occupational testing, selection, appraisal, vocational assessment, and management development. He is a Graduate Member of the British Psychological Society, and Associate Member of the Institute of Personnel & Development. 'Informative... Points for discussion and case studies are prominent throughout... the case studies are highly relevant and good.' *Progress/NEBS Management Association.*

154pp illus. 1 85703 117 2. 2nd edition.

How to Manage a Sales Team
John Humphries

The quality of a sales team can be crucial to the success of an organisation, especially in the fiercely competitive marketplace of the 1990s. Written by a highly experienced training professional, this book meets the need for a practical handbook for every manager responsible for building or leading a sales team. With its useful checklists and case studies, it covers the whole subject from initial planning to recruitment, sales training, motivation and supervision, controlling budgets and forecasts, running sales meetings, and managing the sales function successfully within the organisation as a whole.

160pp illus. 1 85703 079 6.

How to Employ & Manage Staff
Wendy Wyatt

This easy to use handbook will help all managers and supervisors whose work involves them in recruiting and managing staff. Ideal for quick reference, it provides a ready-made framework of modern employment practice from recruitment onwards. It shows how to apply the health & safety at work regulations, how to handle record-keeping, staff development, grievance and disciplinary procedures, maternity and sick leave and similar matters for the benefit of the organisation and its employees. The book includes a useful summary of employment legislation plus a range of model forms, letters, notices and similar documents. Wendy Wyatt GradIPD is an experienced Personnel Manager and Employment Consultant.

128pp illus. 0 7463 0554 0.

How to Know Your Rights at Work
Robert Spicer

Written in clear English, this easy-to-follow handbook sets out everyone's rights at work whether in an office, shop, factory or other setting. It outlines the legal framework, the general duties of employers and employees, the legal scope of 'employment', the contract of employment, pay and deductions, hours of work, absences from work, disciplinary and grievance procedures. Other chapters explain the law of redundancy, union involvement, what happens on the transfer of a business, guarantee payments, redundancy pay, sex and racial discrimination, the rights of expectant mothers, disabled people and past offenders. Health and safety at work is also summarised, and the book is complete with a section on going to an industrial tribunal. Robert Spicer MA(Cantab) is a practising barrister, legal editor and author who specialises in employment law.

144pp illus. 1 85703 172 5. 2nd edition.

How to Master Business English
Michael Bennie

As you communicating effectively? Do your business documents achieve the results you want? Or are they too often ignored or misunderstood? Good communication is the key to success in any business. Whether you are trying to sell a product, answer a query or complaint, or persuade colleagues, the way you express yourself is often as important as what you say. With lots of examples, checklists and questionnaires to help you, this book will speed you on your way, whether as manager, executive, or business student. Michael Bennie is an English graduate with many years' practical experience of business communication both in government and industry. He is Director of Studies of the Department of Business Writing of Writers College, and author of *How to Do Your Own Advertising* in this series.

208pp, illus. 1 85703 129 6. 2nd edition.

How to Master Public Speaking
Anne Nicholls

Speaking well in public is one of the most useful skills any of us can acquire. People who can often become leaders in their business, profession or community, and the envy of their friends and colleagues. Whether you are a nervous novice or a practised pro, this step-by-step handbook tells you everything you need to know to master this highly prized communication skill. contents: Preface, being a skilled communicator, preparation, researching your audience, preparing a speech, finding a voice, body language and non-verbal communication, dealing with nerves, audiovisual aids, the physical environment, putting it all together on the day, audience feedback, dealing with the media, glossary, further reading, useful contacts, index. Anne Hulbert Nicholls BA(Hons) PGCE was a Lecturer in Communications and Journalism in a College of Education for 14 years and now runs seminars and conferences for a publishing company. She has also worked in Public Relations and for BBC Radio.

160pp illus. 1 85703 149 0. 3rd edition.

How to Pass That Interview
Judith Johnstone

Everyone knows how to shine at interview — or do they? When every candidate becomes the perfect clone of the one before, you have to have that extra 'something' to raise your chances above the rest. Using a systematic and practical approach, this How To book takes you step-by-step through the essential pre-interview groundwork, the interview encounter itself, and what you can learn from the experience afterwards. The book contains sample pre- and post-interview correspondence, and is complete with a guide to further reading, glossary of terms, and index. A Graduate of the Institute of Personnel & Development, Judith Johnstone has been an instructor in Business Studies and adult literacy tutor, and has long experience of helping people at work.

128pp illus. 1 85703 118 0. 2nd edition.

How to Keep Business Accounts
Peter Taylor

The third fully revised edition of this easy-to-understand handbook for all business owners and managers. 'Will help you sort out the best way to carry out double entry book-keeping, as well as providing a clear step-by-step guide to accounting procedures.' *Mind Your Own Business*. 'Progresses through the steps to be taken to maintain an effective double entry book-keeping system with the minimum of bother.' *The Accounting Technician*. 'Compulsory reading.' *Manager, National Westminster Bank (Midlands)*. Peter Taylor is a Fellow of the Institute of Chartered Accountants, and of the Chartered Association of Certified Accountants. He has many years' practical experience of advising small businesses.

176pp illus. 1 85703 111 8. 3rd edition.

How to Master Book-Keeping
Peter Marshall

Book-keeping can seem a confusing subject for people coming to it for the first time. This very clear book will be welcomed by everyone wanting a really user-friendly guide to recording business transactions step-by-step. Illustrated at every stage with specimen entries, the book will also be an ideal companion for students taking LCCI, RSA, BTEC, accountancy technician and similar courses at schools, colleges or training centres. Typical business transactions are used to illustrate all the essential theory, practice and skills required to be effective in a real business setting. Peter Marshall has been Tutor in Education at the University of Lancaster and Director of Studies at the Careers College, Cardiff. He has contributed regularly to *FOCUS on Business Education*.

176pp illus. 1 85703 065 6. 2nd edition.

How to Manage Computers at work
Graham Jones

Most books on computers are highly technical, and often tied in to one particular application or product. This book really is different. Assuming no prior knowledge, it is a practical step-by-step guide which puts the business needs of the user first. It discusses why a computer may be needed, how to choose the right one and instal it properly; how to process letters and documents, manage accounts, and handle customer and other records and mailing lists. It also explains how to use computers for business presentations, and desktop publishing. If you feel you should be using a computer at work, but are not sure how to start, then this is definitely the book for you . . . and you don't need an electronics degree to start! 'Bags of information in a lingo we can all understand. I strongly recommend the book.' *Progress/NEBS Management Association*. Graham Jones has long experience of handling personal computers for small business management and is Managing Director of a desktop publishing company.

160pp illus. 1 85703 078 8.

How to Do Your Own Advertising
Michael Bennie

This book is for anyone who needs — or wants — to advertise effectively, but does not want to pay agency rates. Michael Bennie is Director of Studies at the Copywriting School. 'An absolute must for everyone running their own small businesss . . . Essential reading . . . Here at last is a practical accessible handbook which will make sure your product or service gets the publicity it deserves.' *Great Ideas Newsletter (Business Innovations Research)*. 'Explains how to put together a simple yet successful advertisement or brochure with the minimum of outside help . . . amply filled with examples and case studies.' *First Voice (National Federation of Self Employed and Small Businesses).*

176pp illus. 0 7463 0579 6.

How to Write a Press Release
Peter Bartram

Every day, newspapers and magazines are deluged with thousands of press releases. Which stories make an editor sit up and take notice? Why do some press releases never get used? The author knows from more than 20 years' first-hand experience in journalism what turns a release from scrap paper into hot news. This book takes you through every stage of the process from conceiving the story idea, researching the information and writing the release, to distributing it by the most effective means. If you have ever had a press release rejected – or want to win 'free' column inches for your organisation – *How to Write a Press Release* is the handbook for you. Peter Bartram BSc(Econ) is one of Britain's most published business writers and journalists, with more than 2,500 feature articles and seven books to his credit. He edits the magazine *Executive Strategy.*

160pp illus. 1 85703 163 6. 2nd edition.

How to Write a Report
John Bowden

Communicating effectively on paper is an essential skill for today's business or professional person for example in managing an organisation, staffing, sales and marketing, production, computer operations, financial planning, and reporting, feasibility studies and business innovation. Written by an experienced manager and staff trainer, this well-presented handbook provides a very clear step-by-step framework for every individual, whether dealing with professional colleagues, customers, clients, suppliers or junior or senior staff. Contents: Preparation and planning. Collecting and handling information. Writing the report: principles and techniques. Improving your thinking. Improving presentation. Achieving a good writing style. Making effective use of English. How to choose and use illustrations. Choosing paper, covers and binding. Appendices (examples, techniques, checklists), glossary, index. John Bowden BSc(Econ) MSc has long experience both as a professional manager in industry, and as a Senior Lecturer running courses in accountancy, auditing, and effective communication.

160pp illus. 1 85703 124 5. 2nd edition.

How to Start a Business from Home
Graham Jones

Most people have dreamed of starting their own business from home at some time or other; but how do you begin? The third edition of this popular book contains a wealth of ideas, projects, tips, facts, checklists and quick-reference information for everyone — whether in between jobs, taking early retirement, or students and others with time to invest. Packed with information on everything from choosing a good business idea and starting up to advertising, book-keeping and dealing with professionals, this book is essential reading for every budding entrepreneur. 'Full of ideas and advice.' *The Daily Mirror*. 'This book is essential – full of practical advice.' *Home Run.*

176pp, illus. 1 85703 126 1. 3rd edition.

How to Buy & Run a Shop
Iain Maitland

The retail sector is notorious for the number of small shops which fail in their first few years. This step-by-step guide offers hard-hitting advice on running a retail shop, how and where to trade, records and accounts, employment and consumer law, tricks of the trade, and is complete with case studies and references. 'Before going any further, consider his advice.' *Daily Express: Business Plus*. 'Meets a real need for a practical guide for anyone thinking of buying or running a shop. With its clear step-by-step approach it sets out all you need to know.' *Independent Retailer.*

156pp illus. 1 85703 153 9. 3rd edition.

How to Buy & Run a Small Hotel
Ken Parker

'How I wish we'd had proper advice before we took the plunge!' is a frequent cry amongst those providing serviced accommodation. This informative guide meets that demand, and provides a firm base of knowledge on which to enter this competitive business. How to prepare yourself, how to decide what to look for, how to raise finance, where to get professional advice, how to select the right equipment and staff and how to run a hotel at a profit are just some of the key topics comprehensively and expertly covered. 'Also of value to those already involved.' *Business Executive Magazine/ABE.* Ken Parker is an experienced hotelier, freelance journalist and writer, and has extensive experience of managing staff, administration and lecturing.

206pp illus. 1 85703 050 8.

How to Sell Your Business
Robert Ziman

Are you thinking of selling your business? Perhaps you feel it is time for a change, or retirement beckons, or your personal circumstances have changed. Whatever the reasons, you will certainly want to get the best deal. But how do you market a business? What about the timing, method and costs? What about confidentiality, and negotiating with prospective buyers? Written by a business transfer agent with a lifetime's experience, this book shows you step-by-step how to manage the whole process from the beginning, through setbacks, and towards a satisfactory outcome. It is complete with many examples, checklists, sample documents and other essential information to set you on your way.

160pp illus. 1 85703 119 9.

How to Invest in Stocks and Shares
Dr John White

This book has been specially updated to help and guide those with a lump sum or surplus income to invest and who are considering investing all or part of this in quoted securities. Dr John White, an Oxford graduate, is himself an experienced investor and adviser to an investment company. He has a professional background in computers and has produced a range of software for chart analysis. 'User friendly... Contains many practical examples and illustrations of typical share-dealing documents. There are also case studies which give you a feel for your own inclinations about risk versus profit... Demystifies the world of stocks and shares.' *Own Base*. 'Will be a help to private investors... Gives an easy to understand guide to the way the stockmarket works, and how the investor should go about setting up a suitable investment strategy.' *What Investment.*

208pp illus. 1 85703 112 1. 2nd edition.

How to Retire Abroad
Roger Jones

Increasing numbers of people are looking for opportunities to base their retirement overseas — away from many of the hassles of life in the UK. This book meets the need for a really comprehensive and practical guide to retiring abroad — from the initial planning stages, to choosing the right location and property, and adapting to a completely new environment. Such a big change in lifestyle can involve many pitfalls. Written by a specialist in expatriate matters, this handbook will guide you successfully step-by-step through the whole process of finding a new home, coping with key matters such as tax, foreign investment, property, health care, and even working overseas. The book is complete with a country-by-country guide.

176pp illus. 1 85703 051 6.

How to do your own advertising
How to conduct staff apprasiels